SOPHOS

CHARLES BYNUM

THE DIVINE IN ME PUBLISHING, LLC

FOREWORD

There is something magical about a quest, the search for that one entity that can change everything. Many have tried, and the folklore surrounding these efforts are filled with spectacular stories that make for an excellent Hollywood movie. We've seen them: The Da Vinci Code, Raiders of the Lost Ark, The Quest for the Holy Grail…and the list goes on. As a culture in the West, we love the thought of the adventure, we long for the fame and fortune, and we live out our dreams in the fantasies of our minds. But, adventure is much more than just a puzzle to be solved or a long lost artifact to be found.

This book is about a quest that involves all the spectacular events of any quest, except the prize is ironically different and yet the same. It is a prize of unfathomable wealth and beauty but enclosed in sincere simplicity. It is a prize that could solve the world's problems, yet it may be the very cause of all of them. It exists at the core of every living being, yet it seems just beyond their reach. It is a journey that all people are called to embark upon, but few ever finish. It is a quest I challenge you to accept.

It could be that present society is so fascinated with the "prize" of the quest that we miss the purpose of the quest along the way. Learning must be a part of the journey. In this book, Charles Bynum will challenge you to realize that the "...most important thing you must still learn is how to unlearn." It sounds so simple, yet is so difficult to do. It was a struggle for some of the greatest minds in history. To unlearn is to let go of the thought of the "prize" and to become obsessed with the process. To Bertrand Russell, the great philosopher, the quest was more about what he learned along the way and then invested in those he encountered along the journey.

Sophos is an allegory of such a quest by a man in search of the prize but instead finds that the prize is found piece by piece through the process of the journey. This book is written by Charles Bynum, a former student in my Philosophy class, who learned how to give up the "prize" and found (or is finding) his fulfillment in the process of the quest. He engages all of the things in our culture that are deemed "important" or "valuable" by society's standards. He challenges the reader to identify with the main character, who is much like you (and me); in fact, he is you and me. I found this book challenging, while many times wanting to throw it across the room and cry "heretic!" The hardest part is that sometimes the things that upset us the most are the things that need the greatest amount of attention in our lives. Charles Bynum is writing this book, not from a prophetic point of view, but a relative one. It is his story about the quest to know the "truth." Like Bertrand Russell, he found that there may be no perfect path to absolute truth, but his passions have been enriched along the way and his message is a message that will revolutionize any person or society that has "an ear to hear."

This book has the potential to challenge everything you've known to be true (or possibly not true)—if you let it. To both the religious and the non-religious, it will shake you to the core and force you to address things that you may find disagreeable. This book is not a nice little story with a fairytale ending; it is a challenge, which if accepted, will forever change the nature of who you are. It is a challenge with a happy ending…if you are willing and ready to accept it.

There are those who have the ability to hone in on the areas of our life that need consideration and provide that attention. As a former student, Charles allowed me (on many occasions) to be the iron on which he sharpened himself. From that time on, we have spent many hours "sharpening" one another. The writer of Proverbs wrote, "As iron sharpens iron, so one man sharpens another" (Proverbs 27:17). Charles Bynum is, in my opinion, one of those people, and through this book he has definitely helped me sharpen my edge.

Dr. Craig Schroetlin

INTRODUCTION

There comes a time when the world longs for a new story as the old stories have lost their power and no longer speak to the deep need of the people. It is therefore incumbent upon the story teller to speak to that which is operating in the collective mind outside of the awareness of any individual mind manifesting within the collective. It is through this telling that the individual is reconciled with the spirit of the age in which he or she exists. This is, after all, the function of myth...to speak that which cannot be spoken so as to align the individual with that which is known, even though the individual does not yet know he knows it. Sounds like an odd assertion doesn't it?—to tell that which cannot be told to those who know but do not know they know. What manner of nonsense is this? And yet, this nonsense has been a central tenant of the human condition since the beginning of time. It serves a deep need in the human psyche, without which the individual feels himself lost, ungrounded, floating, as it were, in a reality that seems almost unreal, with no firm ground upon which to stand.

We think ourselves beyond the need of myths these days. We think of myths as silly stories of Gods and Goddesses perhaps fighting in the heavens, or lost in their intrigues on Mt. Olympus. Some people view the modern religions as "nothing more than myth," juvenile stories of a God in heaven who will cast us into a pit of hell to suffer eternal torment if we fail to do this or that (though what this or that actually is, is a matter of debate). The problem lies in the idea "Nothing more than myth." This trivializes the power of the myth by confusing the antiquated stories of old with the function they once served in the human psyche. As the human mind progresses, the old stories no longer speak to those darkened places hidden in the mind, thus the stories begin to seem trite or silly. This is not to say that a new story is not needed. A new story *is* needed, for we humans do not function well in the world without one.

The simple fact of the matter is that no myth is to be taken literally; it is not meant to be believed as if it is describing events that "really" happened. Mythological stories do much more than describe events in time. They point to that unknowable something hovering in the periphery of awareness so that the individual can make sense of that which language cannot encapsulate and therefore cannot fully describe. When people pervert the myth by insisting that the stories contained within it actually happened, they miss the point entirely. When this occurs, it marks the beginning of the death of the myth. Soon there rises groups of people insisting that the myth really did happen exactly as told (as with those who believe in a "literal interpretation of the Bible"), and at the same time there develops a growing number of people who believe such stories to be nothing more than quaint fables, entertaining perhaps, but due to the violence people commit in service to these stories, better to live without them. When this occurs, no one can benefit from the power of myth as the stories lose all of the magic, all of the power they once had. They simply lose the ability to inspire the psyche of those for whom they were written. The myth becomes a dead and lifeless thing, utterly useless. To believe that the stories of the myth happened exactly as described kills the myth just as assuredly as the assumption that they are nothing but childish fairytales will kill it. Both strip the myth of power, the first by concretizing the story, the second by trivializing it. In either event, the mind of the reader no longer probes itself, it instead externalizes the myth. A myth externalized is no myth at all. Once the myth has died it may linger on, languishing in the minds of the people, but it is no longer of any use to the psyche, and it therefore tends to do more harm than good.

A time comes for a new myth to replace the old; a new story to speak to the people in such a way as to ground them to their existence. However modern we may think ourselves to be, we still need a myth to guide us, for without it we are lost, wandering aimlessly with no concept of the meaning of the journey, or even the context in which the journey makes itself known. And that is, after all, the true function of the myth, to contextualize the events of our lives such that they begin to make sense to us as opposed to being a random succession of meaningless stuff happening. We human beings need a collective story to help us make sense of our existence.

To tell such a story requires far more than simple story telling. It also requires that the old story that is written in the mind be un-told. And let us not be mistaken about this; there *is* a story operating in your mind of which you are unaware. Every age has such stories. We learn them from the earliest days of childhood. These stories inform and influence everything in the world of the age for which they were written. They serve as a framework within which everything that is to be known is understood, and without which nothing can be understood. They are a kind of societal glue that allows a common experience in reality. They tell us what to think of a thing before it happens by contextualizing all experience such that people operating under the same story will tend toward a similar conceptualization. These stories act as the categorizing structure that is necessary to understand events. They are like the file cabinet of the mind that is needed so that events can be understood, stored and later retrieved. How that filing system is organized influences how we perceive everything in our world. The problem today is that we are operating on a two-thousand year old mythology that simply cannot function in the modern world, cannot reconcile today's human being with the reality in which he finds himself. Thus we attempt to force new experience into the framework of the antiquated filing system, with the resultant frustration that leads many to throw their hands in the air exasperated, and give up, effectively disconnecting themselves from the commonality of experience so crucial to the deep need of the human psyche—for to try to live life without such a story to guide us is a frustrating endeavor.

It is the short-comings of the old story that result in the feeling of isolation and separation that have become the modern human experience—that existential angst gnawing at the mind that we try to deny as we assign purpose and meaning to our lives, yet somehow suspecting that there is no meaning or purpose, as if we are just a random collection of star-stuff moving about in a cold, dark universe convincing itself that it matters despite all evidence to the contrary. The world has changed, and the individual feels lost within it—disconnected and alone; lost in a despair no amount of distraction will quell. The task then is to tell the new story so that it acts as a lifeline to the psyche of the individual drowning in the noise of the world about him, effectively reconnecting him to the other minds floundering about just as lost as he.

With this in mind, we shall un-tell the old story at the same time as we embark upon the telling of the new in the hope that you will see the need to move beyond the old, to embrace that which, though uncomfortable at times, carries with it the potential for a new understanding, and with that new understanding, the restoration of the balance and the sense of peace that has been lost to you. It is a simple story as all such stories must be. It is a story of a man, and it is a story of a woman. What you will find in it is the unknown and unknowable "something" hovering in the periphery of your awareness—the source of your discontent. It is this "something" that must be brought into consciousness, and with it will come the answer to the question you do not yet know how to ask. Presumptuous of me? Perhaps. But no story is ever told until and unless someone presumes the ability to tell it. The proof will be found, not in what I say of the story, but in the story itself. It will either shine a light on those darkened places that the post-modern world has all but forgotten, or it will not.

CHAPTER 1

He sat atop a mountain, shoulder-length black hair waving in the breeze, his vibrant blue eyes staring into the distance, penetrating deeply into whatever they happened upon. His mind observed all that was around him and all that was in him. It was a quiet observation as he gazed upon that which was, devoid of any need for internal dialog. What he saw, he saw. What he heard, he heard. He felt intensely every waft of wind caressing his skin. There was a time when he would have wrapped these experiences in words such that he experienced the words and not the sensations. But no more. Where he had once been a man, he now simply was.

The sun's warm, caressing rays flowed through him exposing the deep places that were once lost to darkness. He smiled. He reflected upon what a long, arduous journey it had been to the top of the mountain. It was a most unusual journey in that it led to the place he had always been, though somehow he had forgotten that he had always been there. "That is the way," he thought, "We forget what is right before us, so lost are we in the minutia, the drama." Now that he had arrived to the place he had always been, he had to make a decision. It was an important decision that meant nothing. It was an unimportant decision that meant everything. It was neither. It was both. "Such is the way of words," he thought. "They say things, but they are never the things they say." It was then that a vision made itself known in his mind. It was a vision of an ancient text, long lost in the vastness of time. He wondered if it ever really existed or if it was but a figment of his imagination, but that thought quickly left him as he recognized the meaninglessness of it. "My mind loves such questions," he thought. "It seeks the tangible through abstraction, though the tangible is never to be found through abstraction." He sighed. What he now knew was something that could not be known in the mind. It could only be known in the marrow of his bones. And there he knew that the real would never be known through words, even though the real could never be known without them. It seemed to him that words pointed to a truth that must be realized through experience. They carry a person to that point where one must leave the words if one is to know. "People get lost in the words," he thought, "They miss the experience of that which is real, and they experience the words instead." This manifested, as he was now beginning to see, as a constant dialog in the mind in which one describes experiences to oneself without really living them. The trick, if it can be called a trick since every child is born knowing how to do this and only forgets when his conditioning forces upon him the demands of his society, is to use the words to bring one to an experience, then move beyond the words fully into the experience itself. He thought about the learning of language, and how it carries with it certain rules that trap one in the language such that one no longer knows how to experience anything without it. He remembered a time, not so long ago, when he met a man who became a dear friend, a man who helped him see this little known fact about language, and helped him to become aware of how trapped in words he really was. The friend asked him to sit silently and see how long he could remain still without any word coming into his mind. "See if you can think without them," the friend instructed.

The man tried this and soon found that within seconds words came into his mind. He realized that he no longer knew how to think without them. Every thought that ever manifested in his mind did so as a word. Any experience that did not have a word attached to it found no fertile soil in which to root in his mind, and though it existed, it was to him as if it didn't. He also began to realize that he could not form memories without words, and that as such, anything that he may experience beyond the limitations of the language, became something that, because he lacked the words with which to file it in memory, was completely forgotten as though it never happened.

He remembered his friend asking him if he thought that odd. "People who speak other languages have words for experiences that you English speaking people do not have. And you have words for certain experiences that they do not have. For example, the Germans have a word 'weltanshauung,' which roughly translates to a world view or a conceptual framing that informs a person's view of reality. But even though I try to explain the word in English, there is an essence the word points to that my English translation misses entirely. As such, the feeling or the experience of 'weltanshaaung' is one the German people can have but you cannot simply because you do not have a word for it, therefore if you do happen to feel it, you have no way of knowing you did so."

The man learned that if one relies too heavily upon words, one misses those experiences that lie beyond them. Thus he began his practice of thinking without them, fully feeling even that which he was unable to describe. When the picture of the ancient text popped into his mind, he knew that asking the question "Did it ever really exist" was a question that, if answered, would add nothing to his experience. The words *were* there—right there in his mind. In that sense they absolutely existed. They revealed themselves to him and he could read them. To say they "actually" existed or to say they were merely "imagined," made no difference. He thought to himself how strange his bias in favor of that which can be proven to be real—and by "proven to be real" it is meant that others agree that it exists—over images that exist only in his mind. All images exist only in the mind. The real question people are asking, though they are unaware they are doing so, is do they exist in many minds, or do they exist only in one. If the image exists in many, it is presumed to be real. If it exists only in the one, it is presumed to be imagination. "That is just my imagination," are the words that discount what the one mind only can perceive, as if it is less real because only the one mind can see it. Yet every great idea came from just that place—the psyche of someone who saw in his or her mind that which no one else could see. He now knew that even if the text existed "only in his mind," his mind is real, therefore what his mind manifests is also real. He determined he would relax into it and let the text appear to him. The text that he now saw was a text that revealed itself only to those who were ready to see it. He knew this, though he didn't know how he knew it.

The text opened before his eyes, and he began to read...

1. IN THE BEGINNING, ALREADY CONTAINED WITHIN IT WAS THE END, SUCH THAT THERE WAS NO BEGINNING, NOR WAS THERE AN END, ONLY THAT WHICH EVER WAS, FLOWING, PULSING; DOING THAT WHICH THE ALWAYS IS HAD ALWAYS DONE. NO DIVISION, NO TIME, NO PARTS, JUST THE UNIFIED WHOLE BREATHING, BEING.

2. THE EARTH WAS WITHOUT FORM, FOR THE ALWAYS IS DID NOT YET FEEL

THE NEED TO IMPOSE FORM. AND AS
THE ALWAYS IS, IS ALL THERE EVER WAS,
THERE WAS NO OTHER MIND THAT
COULD IMPOSE THE ILLUSION OF FORM.

3. THE ALWAYS IS COULD BE AND DO
ANYTHING IT COULD IMAGINE. AND
SO THE ALWAYS IS DECIDED TO PLAY
WITH WHAT ALWAYS WAS, AND TO
DREAM A REALITY INTO BEING. IT IS
THIS DREAM THAT WE THINK OF AS
THE BEGINNING.

4. THE ALWAYS IS DREAMED ITSELF AS
THE MANY THINGS SO THAT WHAT WAS
AND STILL IS THE UNIFIED ONE, BEGAN
TO EXPERIENCE ITSELF AS THE MANY
DIFFERENT THINGS. IT IMAGINED
LIGHT AND DARKNESS AND LIGHT AND
DARKNESS WERE. IT IMAGINED ROCKS
AND MINERALS AND THOSE WERE TOO.
AS IT IMAGINED, SO IT WAS. IN THIS
WAY THE MANY THINGS CAME TO BE.

5. THE ALWAYS IS IMAGINED THE
ELEMENTS, AND FIRE, AIR, WATER

AND EARTH SUDDENLY WERE.
LAND AROSE FROM THE WATER
AND SOON PLANTS AND ANIMALS
WERE. EACH WAS BUT A VARIOUS
MANIFESTATION OF THE UNIFIED
ONE. EACH SEPARATE THING
NOTHING BUT A MANIFESTATION
OF THE ALWAYS IS FEEDING UPON
OTHER MANIFESTATIONS OF THE
ALWAYS IS—LIFE FLOWING OUT OF
THIS AND INTO THAT, AND BACK
INTO THIS AGAIN.

6. CYCLES OF EXISTENCE CAME TO
BE AS THE ALWAYS IS MANIFESTED
AS THE MANY THINGS FOR BRIEF
MOMENTS, EACH ONE FADING AWAY
AND BECOMING OTHER MANY THINGS.
EVERYTHING EBBED AND FLOWED
ACCORDING TO THE BREATH OF THE
ALWAYS IS. NIGHT DISSOLVED INTO
DAY THEN BACK INTO NIGHT AGAIN.
ANIMAL DISSOLVED INTO PLANT
THEN BACK INTO ANIMAL AGAIN.
EVERYTHING MOVED ACCORDING TO
THE RHYTHM OF THE ALWAYS IS.

7. THE ALWAYS IS THEN IMAGINED MALE AND FEMALE, EACH ONE FLOWING INTO THE OTHER AND THEN BACK AGAIN. IT WAS THE ALWAYS IS DOING WHAT IT ALWAYS DOES, PULSING TO ITS OWN RHYTHM, BREATHING, DOING, BECAUSE THAT IS WHAT IT DOES. EVERYTHING IS BUT A PARTICULAR MANIFESTATION OF THE ONE, FLOWING FIRST INTO THIS, THEN INTO THAT.

8. THE ALWAYS IS IMAGINED MAN AND WOMAN, AND MAN AND WOMAN CAME TO BE. MAN AND WOMAN BECAME THE PINNACLE OF THE DREAM OF THE ALWAYS IS, FOR THROUGH THEM THE ALWAYS IS COULD EXPERIENCE ITS CREATION FROM INSIDE THE DREAM. THROUGH MAN AND WOMAN IT COULD LOSE ITSELF IN THE DRAMA OF THE MANY THINGS.

9. AND SO IT WAS THAT THE MAN AND THE WOMAN WERE GIVEN A MIND THROUGH WHICH THEY COULD

KNOW THEMSELVES AS ONE OF THE MANY THINGS, WHILE FORGETTING WHAT THEY REALLY WERE AS AN EXPRESSION OF THE ALWAYS IS. IN THIS WAY, THE DREAMER FORGOT HE WAS DREAMING, AND THE DREAM BECAME KNOWN TO HIM AS REALITY.

10. SOON THE ALWAYS IS GAVE MAN AND WOMAN THE ULTIMATE POWER. IT GAVE THEM THE WORD. THE WORD WAS THE MOST AWESOME OF POWERS, FOR THROUGH IT THE ONE THING COULD BE MADE INTO DIFFERENT THINGS.

11. THE WORD COULD BE USED TO DESCRIBE ALL THINGS, TO COMMUNICATE ALL THINGS, TO UNDERSTAND ALL THINGS. BUT THE WORD COULD NOT BE USED TO COME TO KNOW THE ONE THING.

12. THE ALWAYS IS WONDERED, "IF I LOSE MYSELF COMPLETELY IN THE MANY THINGS, HOW LONG WILL IT TAKE ME TO REMEMBER THE ONE

THING?" SO HE LOST HIMSELF IN THE MANY THINGS, AND FORGOT HIMSELF AS THE ONE THING. IT WAS A DREAM IN WHICH THE DREAMER FORGOT HE WAS DREAMING AS HE MOVED INTO THE DRAMA OF THE MANY THINGS.

13. THE ALWAYS IS LOST HIMSELF IN THE GAME OF HIS DREAM. THE ALWAYS IS LOST HERSELF IN THE OTHER PART OF HER DREAM. IT WAS A DANCE IN WHICH THE ALWAYS IS SOUGHT UNION WITH WHAT IT ALREADY WAS. IT HAD FORGOTTEN WHAT IT ALREADY WAS AND SUBMERGED ITSELF IN THE EXPERIENCE OF THE MANY THINGS.

14. EARTH WAS ITS BODY. PLANTS AND ANIMALS WERE ITS ORGANS, AND MAN AND WOMAN WERE ITS MIND. EACH OF THE MANY THINGS AN INTRICATE PART OF THE WHOLE; EACH COMPLETELY DEPENDENT UPON THE OTHER.

15. THUS THE DREAM BEGAN. HOW WOULD IT END? THIS MATTERED NOT,

FOR IT WAS THE DREAM ITSELF THAT MATTERED.

16. MAN AND WOMAN BEGAN TO THINK, AND THEY USED THE POWER OF THE WORD TO LABEL EACH OF THE MANY THINGS. BUT THEY FOUND THAT TO DO SO MADE NO SENSE, AS THE MANY THINGS WERE NOT MANY THINGS AT ALL, BUT WERE INSTEAD ONE THING IN FLUX.

17. SO IT WAS THAT MAN DEVISED THE WORD TIME. IT WAS THROUGH THE USE OF THE WORD TIME THAT MAN COULD DIVIDE THE FLOW OF THE ONE INTO SMALL INCREMENTS. WOMAN THEN DEVISED THE WORD SPACE, AND NOW SHE COULD CONFINE THE FLOW OF THE ONE INTO THINGS SHE COULD LABEL.

18. MAN AND WOMAN THEN DEVISED WORDS SUCH AS COW AND GRASS AND LIFE AND DEATH. IN THIS WAY THEY COULD SEPARATE WHAT WAS

GRASS-LIFE FLOWING INTO COW-LIFE AND BACK INTO GRASS-LIFE AGAIN, INTO DISTINCT THINGS.

19. THE WORD DEATH WAS MOST HELPFUL, FOR IT AFFORDED THEM AN ILLUSORY SEPARATION THAT MADE THEIR LABELS FUNCTION FOR THEM. NOW THE LIFE THAT WAS IN GRASS ENDED WHEN COW ATE IT. AND THE LIFE THAT WAS IN COW ENDED WHEN IT DECOMPOSED INTO FOOD FOR THE GRASS.

20. THE RHYTHM THAT WAS THE FLOW OF THE BREATH OF THE ALWAYS IS WAS NOW EXPERIENCED BY MAN AND WOMAN AS SEPARATE AND DISTINCT THINGS. SUCH IS THE POWER OF THE WORD.

21. SOON ALL OF THE MANY THINGS HAD A NAME. EACH NAME BUT A REPRESENTATION OF ONE OF THE MANY THINGS, A SYMBOL WITH WHICH MAN AND WOMAN COULD

COMMUNICATE THEIR SEPARATE EXPERIENCES AS IF EXPERIENCES WERE SOMEHOW SEPARATE.

22. MAN AND WOMAN SOON NOTICED PATTERNS IN THE WORDS. OFTEN THEY WOULD FIND THAT, WHEN ONE WORD OCCURRED, ANOTHER WORD SOON FOLLOWED. IT WAS THROUGH THESE PATTERNS THAT THE WORD ASSERTED ITS GREAT POWER.

23. MAN AND WOMAN NOTICED THAT THE WORD DEATH ALWAYS FOLLOWED THE WORD LIFE. THEY FORGOT THAT LIFE AND DEATH DID NOT REALLY EXIST. THEY FORGOT THAT ONLY THE WORDS THEMSELVES EXISTED. IT WAS NO LONGER THE LIFE ENERGY TEMPORARILY EXISTING IN GRASS FLOWS INTO COW THEN BACK INTO GRASS AGAIN. IT WAS NOW GRASS DIED AND WAS NO MORE. COW DIED AND WAS NO MORE. THUS WAS BORN THE CONCEPT OF BEGINNING AND END WHERE BEGINNING AND END NEVER ACTUALLY WERE.

24. MAN AND WOMAN SOON REALIZED THAT THEY TOO WOULD COME TO AN END. IT WAS THEN THAT A NEW SENSATION DEVELOPED IN THE PITS OF THEIR STOMACHS AND MAN AND WOMAN LABELED THIS SENSATION "FEAR." THIS WAS THE TRUE FALL OF MAN. THIS SIGNALED THE BIRTH OF SIN.

25. MAN AND WOMAN WERE NEVER BANISHED FROM THE GARDEN. INSTEAD THEY INVENTED WORDS THAT BECAME MORE REAL TO THEM THAN REALITY ITSELF. THOSE WORDS CREATED THE SENSATION OF FEAR, AND IT WAS FEAR THAT DROVE THEM TO CREATE THE MOST POWERFUL OF ALL WORDS: GOOD AND EVIL.

26. LIFE WAS GOOD; DEATH WAS EVIL. AND WITH THAT THE DOOR SLAMMED SHUT. MAN AND WOMAN HAD BANISHED **THEMSELVES** FROM THE GARDEN.

27. THEY NOW BELIEVED THEMSELVES TO BE SEPARATE THINGS THAT WOULD ONE DAY END. FEAR BECAME THEIR CONSTANT COMPANION. IT WAS SO PREVALENT THEY BEGAN TO GIVE IT MANY DIFFERENT NAMES.

28. INTENSE FEAR BECAME "TERROR". MILD FEAR BECAME "APPREHENSION". FEAR OF WHAT MIGHT HAPPEN IN THE FUTURE BECAME "WORRY". FEAR OVER MAKING A DECISION BECAME "DOUBT."

29. THE AWESOME POWER OF THE WORD TURNED AGAINST MAN AND WOMAN. MAN AND WOMAN NO LONGER EXPERIENCED WHAT IS; THEY INSTEAD EXPERIENCED WORDS THAT ATTEMPTED TO DESCRIBE TO THEM WHAT IS. SOON THEY EXPERIENCED ONLY THE WORDS. THE WORDS BECAME MORE REAL TO THEM THAN THE EXPERIENCE ITSELF.

30. THUS THEY BECAME SLAVES TO THE WORD. BEFORE LONG THE WORD

"I" APPEARED, AND WITH THAT, THE DEVIL ENTERED INTO THE WORLD.

31. IT WAS THEN THAT MAN AND WOMAN BEGAN TO CHANGE. THEY BECAME **A** MAN AND **A** WOMAN. SOON THAT CHANGED INTO **I** AM A MAN, AND **I** AM A WOMAN. WORDS STACKED UPON WORDS UNTIL MAN AND WOMAN FELT THEMSELVES SEPARATED EVEN FROM ONE ANOTHER.

32. EACH BECAME AN "I." THE "I" BECAME PARAMOUNT, AND SERVICE TO **ITS** NEEDS, **ITS** WANTS, **ITS** DESIRES CONSUMED MAN AND WOMAN.

33. THEY WERE NO LONGER **A PART OF** THE WORLD; THEY HAD BECOME ENTITIES THAT WERE **APART FROM** THE WORLD.

34. REALITY BECAME THE LIE, AND THE LIE BECAME REALITY. MAN TURNED AGAINST MAN. WOMAN TURNED AGAINST WOMAN. MAN TURNED AGAINST

WOMAN. WOMAN TURNED AGAINST MAN. EACH SEPARATE "I" SEEKING ITS OWN EXISTENCE IN OPPOSITION TO ALL OTHERS. SUFFERING WAS THE NEXT WORD THAT CAME TO BE.

35. EXISTENCE WAS NO LONGER A CONTINUOUS PROCESS OF EBB AND FLOW. IT WAS NOW A BRIEF PERIOD OF SUFFERING IN WHICH EACH SEPARATE "I" ATTEMPTED TO MAKE THE ILLUSION OF THE WORD REAL IN OPPOSITION TO WHAT REALLY WAS. MAN AND WOMAN THEN COMPARED WHAT THEY THOUGHT LIFE SHOULD BE TO WHAT LIFE IS, AND THEY FOREVER FOUND LIFE AS IT IS LACKING.

36. THUS THE STRUGGLE OF LIFE WAS BORN. IT WAS IN REALITY THE STRUGGLE OF NOTHING MORE THAN SYMBOLS ARRANGED IN SUCH A WAY AS TO CREATE THE STRUGGLE ITSELF. IT WAS ALL AN ILLUSION, AND MAN AND WOMAN LOST THEMSELVES WITHIN IT...

He smiled as these words flowed through him. They were old words, written in some long forgotten past. Perhaps they were never written at all, but he sensed that they had been written somewhere. They spoke a deep truth. And because they spoke this truth, he had a decision to make, though he was in no hurry to make it. From atop the mountain there were but two places left for him to go. He could fly ever upward into the blissful nothingness stretching out above him. Or, he could journey back down the mountain from whence he came and immerse himself in that thing known as life.

An eagle soared screeching its presence into his awareness. He glanced at its majestic beauty carried along by the invisible hand of the winds, and he longed to be one with it. Eagles have much to offer, he thought…but so do serpents.

It was then that he heard something slithering in the bushes at his feet. He glanced downward and found the serpent approaching. It stared into his eyes, and then it spoke.

"Are you man, or are you woman?" it asked.

"I am," the man replied.

"Are you God, or are you mortal?" it asked.

"I *am*," he replied again, more sternly than before.

"I see," the serpent said. "Then what say ye? Do you soar with your eagle? Or will you follow me down to the valley below?"

The man paused, and then he spoke.

"Countless times have I followed you, and each time I find myself back where I began. Yet should I choose to follow you this time, I will not act in opposition to you. I will instead walk beside you, for that is how I wish it to be."

"You know," the serpent replied, "those in the valley fear and despise me. Should you walk with me, they will also fear and despise you. They may not be ready for you. They are frightened and confused. People love their fear, and they will not be quick to let it go. They exist in their fear as their fear exists in them. The only thing they fear more than fear is freedom from fear. To them, fear is life. To let go of fear feels like death."

"They may not be ready, but I am," he replied. "The eagle soars high above me, and you slither down below, yet I am beholden to you both. I must bring the eagle to the valley floor, and the serpent must soar in the sky. But the time has not yet come. I have much to consider and I am tired and in need of rest. I shall sit here for now. Perhaps I shall slither. Perhaps I shall fly. Perhaps both. Perhaps neither. I have a decision to make; or rather, there is a decision to be made. Perhaps the decision will make me. I shall wait until the decision is ready then I shall follow its will. So slither off to your valley serpent, and trouble me no more."

With that, the serpent slithered back down the mountain as the man sat smiling in the silence. The sky called him into the blissful nothingness that was his true nature. And yet, the valley called him also. He thought about descending, about returning to the valley, for there was much suffering there. That suffering cried out to him, pleading with him to bring into the valley that which he had learned so that the suffering might be eased. He was troubled, his soul disturbed.

He longed to ease the pain of the people of the valley, but he was not sure what he could do. He felt a hand press gently upon his shoulder. He turned his head to find his old friend Mara standing beside him.

"Thinking of going back?" Mara asked.

"I am," the man replied.

Mara picked up a small pebble and tossed it down the side of the mountain. They silently watched it tumble and bounce its way out of view.

"You are tired, my friend," Mara spoke softly, kindly. "Why not enjoy the rest you have earned?"

"I *am* tired," he replied. "But I feel drawn to them. They need me."

"Oh, they will be fine without you," Mara replied. "How many times have you sat atop this mountain, and how many times have you returned? And for what? To end up back here yet again? They will find their way. They have no need of you."

"Perhaps," he answered. "But I have need of them."

"Let me remind you of what it was like the last time," Mara said, and he waved his hand. As he did, visions danced before the man's eyes.

"Behold," Mara continued, "This was you in the valley before, entering into that strange method they have of imposing their insanity upon all who enter there. It is that which they call childhood."

The man watched and he did behold. He beheld the child. He remembered the many ways in which the people of the valley, in a most loving and kind way, did great violence to the child. He watched as the parents taught the child the importance of learning to be that which he was not, and they taught him the great sin of being what he was. He saw countless teachers and others of authority as they coerced and cajoled the boy into being that which they believed a boy *should* be. He saw teaching and training in the skill of learning *what* to think rather than *how* to think. He witnessed those who taught the boy "to do" rather than "to be". He saw the child struggle with these lessons, trying to please those he loved so that he might be loved. He saw love dangled like bait before the boy's eyes, and he saw the ever-present rod eagerly waiting to inflict pain should the child resist. He saw a child whose body was well-fed but whose soul was starved. He watched as the child entered adolescence and railed against the harm being done to him. Until, at last, the child wearied from the struggle and relented, assuming his false identity as a role to be played, losing all memory of the human being he truly was. The child grew into a broken and hollow shell of a man. He cried.

"That is the way down there," Mara said. "They love the illusion and deny the reality. Then they hate themselves for it. They force everyone to participate in the lie. Why do that to yourself again?"

The man breathed deeply, then he spoke. "I will not go back this time as a child. This time I shall go as the man I now am."

"Ah, then you will be the ruler over them all—the 'master of the valley'?"

The man smiled. "You know better than that," he replied. "I will not lord over them. I shall serve them."

"Oh, but they will surely kill you," Mara stated gravely. "You will frighten them. The illusion is so very important to those who live in the shadow of the lie. Should you dare speak the truth to them, they will despise you for it."

The man smiled again and shook his head slowly. "What you say may very well be true, my friend. But you well know that I must act according to my nature, as you must act according to yours. You serve them with deceit, I serve them with truth. They need what we each have to teach them. Without you, I can do nothing. Without me, there is nothing to do."

Mara smiled. Love overwhelmed him. A tear formed in his eye. "I do so love them," he said.

"I know you do my friend, even if they do not. One might be inclined to believe that you love them more than I. For they project onto you every horrible thing that they deny exists in themselves, and they think you hate them and mean them harm. But the truth of your love is unchanged regardless of the opinions of those in the valley. You serve them well."

"Perhaps," Mara replied. "But I think your love is the greater. For you will give them the answers they seek, and they will hate you for it. They think they love peace, but they love suffering more. They blame me for the evil they do. But they will blame you for the evil they are."

The man stood and hugged his friend. As he did, Mara vanished as if he never was. The decision was made in that no decision was really made—it had all been decided long before. Everything was as it must be. The time had come. He began his descent down the mountain.

CHAPTER 2

"I am Sophia the keeper of the gate. I am the space between the thought without which no thought could exist. I am the silence from which all sounds are born. I am the darkness without which no light can shine. I am the nothingness from which all things come to be. What seek ye here?"

"I wish to enter the valley below," the man replied.

"Who are you?" Sophia asked.

"I am man," he replied.

"You seek to trespass my gate that you might wander in my womb that is the valley below?" she asked.

"I do."

"Who sent you?"

"He with whom thou art locked in eternal embrace sent me."

She smiled. "So, he wishes to impregnate my valley with *your* essence, does he?"

"He does."

Sophia thought for a moment. "I will consent to this," she said. "But you will need a guide."

"What need have I of a guide?" the man protested.

"You need a guide," Sophia answered sternly. "You will be allowed to enter, but you may not speak. You may observe, but you may not interact. You may search for the one. When you find him, you must return to me. I will have the final say."

The man frowned. "I do not understand these words you spe…"

"You will, in time," she interrupted. "You, the man who climbed the mountain will now wander amidst those who still suffer. You will not like what you find there. For in them you will find the truth of you."

The man wondered what she meant by these words. "I know the truth of me," he replied.

"Do you?" she asked. "If that is so, there will be nothing for you there." She stared deeply into his eyes and smiled that painful smile of one who knows that to which the other is blind. "That which you think you know, you know not," Sophia said. Her words were more a pleading than a statement. She let out a heavy sigh. "But this is as it should be. My rules are simple. No one is to see you. No one is to know you are there. You may wander about, but you are not to let your presence be known. You are there to learn."

The man stared at her in disbelief. "Who are you to tell me what

I know or what I am to do?" he asked. "Besides, I come to teach the great secret to those who have not yet realized it."

Sophia's eyes narrowed; her voice grew stern. She knew what she had to do, though it pained her to do it. "Teach?" she mocked. "You think you have something to teach? You? The man who, though he stares endlessly at the reflections in the mirror, cannot see himself reflected there? Hah! You look *at* rather than *in*... man. But I see you. I see that which you do not. That which you think you know, you know not. You, the enlightened and exalted one? Hah! You are the darkness who thinks himself to be the light. I know why you are here, and enter my valley you must, for that is how it was meant to be. Mara shall be your guide. Mara will show you that which you must see."

"I have no need of a guide," the man protested.

"But you will have one all the same," Sophia snapped.

The gate stretching across the path beckoned the man to enter. "Mara awaits you on the other side," Sophia said.

"This is not how I wanted this," the man said feebly. His knees grew weak and his body trembled. Doubt entered his mind.

"This is how it will be," Sophia said. "You must agree to my terms or the gate will slam shut and you will not be allowed in."

A battle now raged in the man. He longed for the valley, yet he did not want these conditions. He turned against himself and relented—a useless gesture as men are prone to do.

"I will do as you ask," he said in resignation.

Sophia spoke. "You who have seen so much, and yet you see

nothing. Go now! Enter my valley; wander in my womb. We shall see what truth your essence will bring. For you are man, and I am woman. You are the light, and I am the dark. You think your light is all there is for you know not how to value the darkness. You are the seed, and I am the soil. You think your seed is all there is for you know not how to value the earth. You know much man, but you do not know all. That which you do not know can only be realized through me. I say go now. Do as you must. Violate me as you are compelled to do for that is the nature of you." She stared into his eyes, locked in a battle in which her anger stirred his.

He felt his power growing within him, and with that his words grew bold. "You are mine woman, and I shall do with you as I will."

Sophia faltered, but only for a moment. She did not want what she knew must be. She swallowed hard and gathered her courage. Her sacrifice was necessary to save the man, and she knew it. "And I know you, Man!" Sophia spat back at him. "You are the great Amartanon. This is the name you have earned and it is the name I now bestow upon you. It will follow you wherever you may wander. I will allow this transgression you wish to perpetrate against me. You may do with me as you will. For I love you and value you as you are unable to love and value me. You tear me from you, cast me aside and act as if I do not exist. But you are a fool, for only a fool would believe he could rip his shadow from him. And you think this is love? You think yourself to be holy? You are not what you believe yourself to be, and the truth of that will soon be known. You seek to save that which cannot be saved while ignoring that which you can save. Behold the fool!" she shouted while waving her hand as if speaking before a crowd. "All hail the fool Amartanon," she mocked while bowing before him. "You are lost in your arrogance—you who have climbed the mountain and now think you know all. You are but a reflection of that which you believe yourself to be. You know not the nature of your soul."

He now hated her. "It did not have to be this way," he protested. "But you have created this. You, woman, made me do this. I desired entrance into your valley; yet you set conditions and forced my hand. Do not for a minute think that I am anything other than what I know myself to be. I *am* the light. And I will carry the light that is me into your valley. You set your conditions and I agreed. Then you mocked me. Now I refuse to be bound by any condition set by you. You have no power over me. You are mine to do with as I will. You will either like it, or you will shut your mouth because you have nothing to say that I want to hear."

"Oh you mighty man," she replied, her voice dripping with contempt. "You esteem yourself far too highly. I have now changed my mind. You will not enter here—for I despise you."

"It is too late, woman," he protested. "I have no need of your permission. You are here to serve me and that is what you will do. I will transgress your gate and all that is in it and you can do nothing to stop me." He moved toward the gate.

Sophia jumped in front of him barring his way.

"Step aside, woman," the man growled. "I will not be denied."

Sophia stared at him unwavering, saying nothing, her eyes fixed in a steely resolve. He stared into her eyes, and despite her anger, he saw there both fear and love. Her gaze reached into him touching something deep inside. He felt the pain of what he was about to do, but he could not help but do it. Yes, Sophia had touched something in him, but the thing she touched was something he did not know to exist. Doubt gave him pause. His eyes betrayed him for a brief second. He wavered. Then anger raged within and his pride brought him back.

"I will take what I want, woman," he said as his anger raged to a roiling boil. He grabbed her by the arms and threw her to the ground. He then stepped on her and stomped toward the gate leaving her bleeding behind him. Sophia cried in anguish.

"This violence you have done me shall haunt you for all your days," she shouted after him as he walked away.

"You are dead to me," he shouted back and he spat angrily upon the ground. Sophia's heart broke. Her blood spilt into the earth beneath her. Her torn clothing hung loosely from her body, her matted hair draped across her shoulders.

With that the act was consummated. The gate swung open and the man did enter her valley. Sophia lay on the ground weeping. He felt something stir in him. It was a sense of shame that betrayed him and betrayed what he really was as opposed to what he thought himself to be. He shook off this feeling; buried it deep within him so that it was as if it was not nor had ever been. It was forgotten. He turned his back to her and into the valley he did go. The light now consumed the dark and darkness was no more.

CHAPTER 3

He found Mara sitting on a rock beside the path. A crow cawed in a nearby tree. A chill ran down Amartanon's spine.

"I see you're going back." Mara said to him.

"I am," he replied.

"And Sophia?"

"What about her," he snapped.

"She won't be so easily defeated," Mara answered.

"She is dead to me. I have no need of her. To need her is weak and I am strong."

"All hail the great Amartanon!" Mara said mockingly.

"That is not my name," he protested.

"Ah, but it is," Mara answered, "It is the name Sophia bestowed upon you, and it is the name you shall now carry. It shall be your cross. For it is the name of he who missed the mark."

He stared at Mara with disgust. "You may call me any name you wish. It is of no consequence to me."

"The enlightened one has entered the darkness!" Mara shouted, his words sounding playful, yet scathingly sarcastic.

"I have come," Amartanon stated sternly.

"Who are you?" Mara asked.

"You know full well who I am," Amartanon replied. "Perhaps I should ask, who are you?"

"I am he who is known by many names," Mara answered. "Some call me Mara. Some call me Satan. Some call me Maya. Some call me Lucifer. But I prefer to think of myself as *you*."

Amartanon did not like this so he did not hear it.

Mara continued. "I have passed through the canal and into the light. I come from the darkness for I was the darkness and into the light I was born. I am that which you seek to overcome. I am the nemesis. I am the opposition. I am the anti-you."

"I have no need of you, Mara," Amartanon said.

"Perhaps not," Mara replied. "But you are now bound to me."

"The valley beckons me, and to them I shall go."

Mara smiled. "You know that I will unleash all the forces of darkness against you?"

"That is as it must be," Amartanon answered.

"Is it?" Mara asked. "I wonder. But then, you are the enlightened one who climbed the mountain. Surely you must know." Mara was mocking him, and Amartanon did not like it.

"I do, and they need me. But I have no need of you," he snapped.

"Oh, you need me little man," Mara said. "You need me and I will be with you. Let us commence on this great journey you have chosen. We shall see the terror that awaits us."

"You know not that of which you speak, Mara. Get thee behind me."

"Perhaps not," Mara replied. "But you know not that which you do."

Amartanon stared at Mara perplexed. "I do not understand you, Mara," he said. "But that is of no consequence. I must follow this path down to the valley below. If you are to be with me, so be it. But do not interfere."

Mara nodded in agreement, and with a grandiose gesture extended his arm while bowing in feigned reverence. "After you, m'lord," he said and the two walked the lonely path down into the valley.

They walked in silence. Amartanon resented this presence with him, but Mara refused to leave his side. They wandered down the winding path, descending lower and lower into the valley below. A stream bubbled along beside them. Amartanon carried a knapsack with some food and a few belongings; Mara carried nothing as it seemed that Mara would need nothing. Amartanon wondered about this, but said nothing. It was then that he heard a rustling sound in the bushes beside the path. He paused, but he did not hear it again. He stooped down to investigate, and as he pulled the leaves of the bushes aside, he saw hiding there a white cat. Or at least it had once been a white cat. It was now grey and dingy from neglect. It was scratched and wounded, with dried blood matted into its fur in numerous places about its body.

"Look at this," Amartanon said, and Mara turned to peer over his shoulder.

"It's hurt," he said. Mara said nothing; he merely nodded.

Amartanon reached down to pet the cat, but the animal cowered and hissed so he quickly withdrew his hand. The cat had apparently been lying there for quite some time. Its ribs protruded through its fur indicating that it was starving. Amartanon retrieved a few bits of dried meat from his knapsack and laid it before the wounded creature. The cat struggled to its feet, apparently in great pain, and it cautiously approached the food, clearly terrified of the two strangers. Amartanon saw that the animal feared being attacked while eating, but its hunger proved greater than its fear. It ate nervously, keeping its eyes fixed on the two. Amartanon walked to the stream and filled a small bowl with water and brought it to the cat. The cat drank as if dying of thirst. It eagerly lapped up the water from the dish, and then turned back to the food. When all of the food was consumed, Amartanon laid more before it and the cat ate that too.

"Someone has abused this animal," Amartanon said.

"It would appear so," Mara replied.

Amartanon cautiously extended his hand toward the cat now that he had fed the animal, but it hissed and swatted at him, its claws scratching his hand.

"She has been badly hurt by those who were supposed to care for her," Mara said. "Perhaps we should leave her here."

Amartanon wondered how Mara could say this as if he knew with certainty what had happened to the cat, but the thought quickly left his mind. "I will not leave her here," he protested.

"What can you do?" Mara asked. "You cannot carry the creature. She won't let you touch her. It would appear that she is too weak to travel, and even if she could walk, it is not likely that she will follow us."

"Then we shall stay here with her until she recovers strength enough to go with us," Amartanon said.

"What about your journey into the valley?" Mara asked.

"What value is there in journeying into the valley if I leave this creature to die?"

"But it is just a cat," Mara said.

"She is a living being," Amartanon answered. "And she is in pain. We will take the time to nurse her to health. I will care for her, feed her, and provide her with water. Perhaps she will come to trust me."

"I don't know about that," Mara said. "But I suppose if she regains enough of her strength, she may follow you. She will most likely run off the first chance she gets."

"Either way," Amartanon replied, "we will stay here and nurse her back to health." He sat beside the wounded animal tossing her bits of meat that she quickly devoured. "We shall spend the night here," he continued. "It is getting late anyway. Let us rest and see how this animal feels in the morning."

"Well, aren't you the walking, talking contradiction?" Mara said.

"What do you mean?" Amartanon asked, his attention fixated on the cat.

"It doesn't matter," Mara replied. "I suppose this is as good a place as any to bed down for the night. There is tall grass here near the stream. It should provide some comfort."

The two sat beside the cat, resting and caring for the injured animal. Amartanon continued tossing bits of meat and the cat ate ravenously. Soon night fell, and the two went to sleep.

The following morning, Amartanon awoke to find the cat curled up near him, resting but a few feet away. He reached out to pet the animal but she hissed her displeasure, letting him know that she would not let his hand come near. He wondered what manner of abuse the poor thing had suffered—abuse that only she knew. He was pleased that the cat stayed with him through the night. It was a good sign that gave him hope that, though the animal did not trust him yet, perhaps she one day would. He determined that if the animal followed him he would continue to care for her.

"I see you are awake," Mara said.

Amartanon looked over to Mara. "I am," he said.

"Sleep well?"

"I did."

"You know, that cat might slow us down on this journey of yours," Mara continued. "You're not actually thinking of taking her with us are you?"

"If she chooses to follow, I will care for her," he answered.

Mara shook his head. "Why do you want a cat tagging along?"

"It's not that I want a cat tagging along, but the cat came along. Nothing happens by chance. Everything happens for a reason."

Mara sighed. "Not that old silliness," he said. "Nothing happens by chance...bah! Things just happen. Why do people always seek some mystical reason?"

"You may be right," Amartanon said. "or you may be wrong. I have no way of proving you wrong any more than you can prove yourself to be right. But let's say you are correct. Let's assume that everything that happens is nothing but random events. Then the random thing that is happening now is that I am going to care for this cat. You may say of that anything that you wish. Do you think it a mere random happening now?"

"Not now," Mara replied. "You are choosing it."

"I see," Amartanon answered. "Then you are saying that some things just happen, and others happen for a reason."

"I suppose that *is* what I am saying," Mara answered resignedly, fully aware of the fact that what Amartanon just said made no sense at all. He wanted to point this out to him but thought better of it, thinking it futile to argue with a man who knows everything.

"How do we distinguish one from the other?" Amartanon asked, desiring to press his point.

Mara stared at him saying nothing, annoyed that he insisted on pursuing this discussion.

"We can assume that this cat showed up because she was in need of care and was hopeful that we would care for her. Is that not reason enough?" Amartanon asked.

"Why are you doing this?" Mara asked. "What's the point in continuing this?"

"I think everything happens for a reason and you are a fool to think otherwise."

"It is *your* journey," Mara replied.

"It *is* my journey," Amartanon insisted. "And if I remember correctly, I didn't ask you to join me. The cat, however, I do want to join me. Perhaps *you* happened for no reason."

"Ah," Mara said smiling. "You may be correct on that assumption. But I think not."

"You speak in circles, Mara," Amartanon said.

"And you suffer from the disease of knowledge," Mara snapped. "Since you know everything, you are incapable of learning anything."

Amartanon looked upon Mara with disgust.

"I suppose *you* know everything then?" he asked.

"I know only the one thing, and that is far more than you know." Mara answered.

"And what is this one thing?"

"I know only that I know nothing," Mara replied.

Amartanon again shook his head. "I grow tired of this nonsense," he said. "Let us be on our way."

He stood, gathered his knapsack, and the two began walking down the path that led into the valley. After walking a few yards,

Amartanon stopped and turned to look behind him. The cat stood staring at them. After a few moments she followed, but she kept her distance; her wary gaze fixed on Amartanon. This pleased Amartanon and he retrieved a few morsels of food from his sack and laid them on the ground for the cat to eat. He took a few steps back and the animal approached cautiously. When she felt that it was safe to do so, she quickly devoured the food, then turned to watch them. Amartanon and Mara started walking and the cat followed. Amartanon smiled.

Mara, noticing this, spoke, "Do you think that this act of kindness makes you a good person?" he asked.

Amartanon looked at Mara puzzled. "Truthfully, I never thought about that. It is not about being good. It is about expressing who I am. The cat is in need, and she came to me. I am helping her because this is what I want to do."

"But you do it because it makes you feel good to do so. If it didn't make you feel good, you wouldn't do it," Mara said.

"I don't think that is true," Amartanon replied. "Although you are correct that it makes me feel good to do this, I didn't do it for that purpose. I did it because that is the man I am. I think that when a person gives with no expectation of anything in return, not even the good feeling one gets from doing it, that is the greatest expression of kindness—the only true expression of kindness, actually. Why do you want to make it into something selfish?"

"I don't," Mara answered. "I was simply curious and I wanted to know if you would care for the cat if doing so did not bring you pleasure."

"I cannot answer that," Amartanon said, "because doing so *does* bring pleasure, for me and for the cat, therefore it is not possible to care for her without experiencing pleasure. But I still insist that my pleasure is not what drives me to do it."

"Did it please you to do what you did to Sophia?" Mara asked.

Amartanon stopped. The question angered him. "I did what I had to do to enter this valley," he said. "That woman tried to prevent my entry and I could not allow that."

"But you didn't answer my question. Do you feel good about having done it?"

Amartanon resumed walking as he pondered the question. "No, I don't," he answered. "I wish there had been another way, but there was not. I did what was necessary, but truthfully, I am not proud of it."

"I see," Mara said.

"Why do you ask such questions?"

"Because I am trying to understand you," Mara answered. "One moment you are cruel to Sophia, the next you are caring for a neglected cat. It seems inconsistent to me, that's all."

"And I am attempting to understand you, Mara," Amartanon said. "You claim that things simply happen with no reason behind them, and yet you now seek reasons for everything. My experience has been that the reasons behind events are not always readily apparent, but they make themselves known in time."

"And mine is that through time you weave a meaning into that which has no meaning at all."

"If that is so, then what would be wrong with it? If it makes life more pleasant, then isn't that a good thing?"

"I don't know," Mara answered. "I suppose living in a fantasy could conceivably be more pleasant than living in reality."

"Then I must ask," Amartanon replied, "who is it that determines what reality 'really' is? Yours could be the illusion and mine could be the more accurate description. There exists no observer standing outside of all reality who can answer that question—no one to say that you are correct and I am mistaken. We are all caught within *this* reality and we must make our observations within it too. I have learned that it is through the act of choosing that reality comes to be. Therefore I choose meaning. You are free to choose random events with no meaning. Either choice is valid. I make the one that brings into being the reality I think preferable."

Mara said nothing more. The two continued along the path leading down into the valley. They walked through the day, the cat following cautiously behind. Amartanon felt himself to be a part of the valley. Each tree, bird or flower—even the cat—seemed to him to be an expression of himself. He felt connected to everything around him in some inexplicable way. He felt the cool breeze and the warmth of the bright sunlight on his face. He felt himself to be at peace, almost dream-like, yet there was something not quite settled within him. But this was so distant from his mind that he was not troubled by it. In fact, he didn't even feel it, or rather, he was not consciously aware of the fact that he was feeling it. But it was there just the same, feeling him.

CHAPTER 4

"It will be dark soon," Mara said. "The sun hangs low in the sky. Soon it shall fall from its lofty perch."

"I see that," Amartanon replied. "Night came sooner than I anticipated. We must push onward. Perhaps we will find a village soon."

No sooner had these words left his mouth did they round a bend and there before them stood a village. The sun had now dipped beneath the horizon and darkness descended, but the village was brightly lit. Electric light glowed in the darkness such that night was as day, an artificial day that was no "day" at all. This disrupted the cycles of existence that the villagers once knew, so much so that they no longer felt themselves pulsing to the natural rhythms of life. They now pulsed to a mechanical rhythm instead—a relentless, incessant droning of life that drove them on and on. This light caused the people of the village to never know night as night. They only knew night as numbers on a clock. And to them day was nothing more than the very same numbers repeated.

Amartanon beheld the people of the village and he did wonder as they scurried about; one heading off this way, another heading off that way. He witnessed busy people doing busy things. He wondered what it was each was doing; why were they in such a hurry? As he entered the village, he came upon one of the villagers and he spoke.

"Excuse me good sir," he said. "Might I have a word with you?"

The villager looked up at Amartanon confused by this unwanted interruption, and then he glanced nervously at his watch. "I suppose I could speak to you for a moment," he said, his words fast and staccato. "I am however in a hurry and I do not have much time. I have a very important thing to do."

Amartanon smiled a pleasant smile to the villager. "May I ask why the people of this village are running to and fro?"

This villager looked up at Amartanon as if he had been asked the stupidest question he had ever heard. "They are all doing the things that must be done," he replied. "There are so many things to do, and so little time in which to do them."

"You said that you have an important thing to do?"

"I do," the villager answered.

"And you are in a hurry to do it?"

"Why yes," he replied. "I must get it done soon...I am late already."

"What happens when the important thing is done?" Amartanon asked.

"I will then do the next important thing," the villager said.

"And what makes these things that you do important?"

"They are important because they are to be done. They must be done for that is the way."

"And what if you choose not to do them?"

The villager stared at Amartanon perplexed. "To not do is the one thing that is never done," he answered. The villager again looked nervously at his watch. "I must leave you now, for I am late," he said, and he turned and scurried off to do the thing he felt must be done.

"What strange people," Amartanon said to Mara.

"I once knew a man," Mara replied, "who stared into a mirror yet he never saw himself reflected there."

This irritated Amartanon. "You say such foolish things Mara. I wish you would stay on subject. Why do you suppose these people act in this way?"

Mara smiled a knowing smile, but as Amartanon didn't know, he didn't see. "They do what they do because they believe they must do it," he said.

"Why do they believe they must do these things?"

"Because to them, to *do* is to *be*. They cannot imagine anything else because to them they are nothing if they do not do."

Amartanon wandered through the village with Mara walking beside him. The people of the village saw the two but took little notice of them. To them, Amartanon and Mara were not organic, living beings with whom the villagers might interact. They did not see the two as people so much as they saw them as an obstacle standing between them and that which they believed must be done. That is the way of people who live by the demands of the clock—to them other people become cogs in the machine, as they themselves become cogs in the machine. Time becomes a commodity that forever seems in short supply as if time was a thing that one possessed. Human interaction is thus reduced to a transaction, not a true experience of other, but instead an interaction of parts subservient to a greater purpose—what Amartanon suspected was an economic purpose.

"Why do they choose to live like this?" Amartanon asked.

"They do not realize they are choosing it," Mara replied. "They think this is what life has chosen for them. Do you see that tower over there?"

Amartanon looked up, and in the distance he beheld the tallest tower in the village. Upon it was the face of a huge clock staring down upon the villagers, imposing its will upon them, commanding them to do and to keep doing. Its presence was felt everywhere and by everyone.

"That," Mara continued, "is what drives them. They have invented increments with which they divide that which is into that which is not. That clock has become their God. They worship the clock, and they do that which the clock demands of them. Because of this, they have built this most beautiful village. But they do not see the village. They have so little time, you see. They cannot spare any of that time to actually see the beauty around them. They see only the demands of the clock."

"Why don't they stop?" Amartanon asked.

"Because they no longer see themselves as what they *are*. They see themselves as what they *do*. They are no longer human *beings*; they are now humans *doing*."

Amartanon paused to consider Mara's explanation. He felt troubled by this. He could not understand why the villagers would invent increments of time, then convince themselves that they had little of this stuff they called time, and then act in accordance to the demands that only existed because they had themselves created this illusion.

"Do they ever stop?" he asked.

"They stop only to rest, and they only do that because they must," Mara answered. "But they are never free. Even while resting their minds are plagued with what the clock will demand of them once they awaken. Their sleep is thus disturbed and troubled. They are in a constant state of dis-ease."

Amartanon's heart ached. He wanted to tell the villagers to stop doing. But he knew that it was useless. The words he longed to say were words that could not be heard.

"Don't be troubled," Mara reassured him. "This is the way of these people. They scurry about doing things they do not like so they can be given tiny pieces of paper that they then use to buy things they do not need. They want. But as soon as they get what they want, they want more. They are never satisfied. They are forever striving for that 'something' they think awaits them sometime in the future. They live for the day when they will, at long last, have all of their wants satisfied. They think that then, on that magical day, they will at last be happy. But, poor souls, that day never comes."

Amartanon thought about this. "But," he said, "That day could be right here and right now if they would just stop doing for a few moments."

"That is true," Mara answered. "But they do not see this. They were taught when they were young to go to school so they might be trained on how to do the various things that need to be done. They went to school and they learned. Then they went to secondary school and they learned more. Some went on to university and learned even more. Then they entered the busy bustle of constantly doing, constantly purchasing shiny new things that they never have the time to enjoy. They think that the more shiny things they have, the greater their worth. Thus, they are always empty, never do they feel full."

"There must be something that can be done for them," Amartanon protested.

"No, there is not. Look in this building over here," he said as he led Amartanon to an old decrepit building, worn and neglected. They peered in the window and there they saw lying about old villagers who were sick and weary, as old and as run-down as the building that housed them.

"You see," Mara said. "These are the villagers who have grown too old and too sick to continue doing. They have ignored their own bodies to the point that their bodies have now failed them. They are warehoused here, forgotten, because they can no longer do. To no longer do means that this village no longer finds value in them. This is what awaits these people, yet none of them think it will ever happen to them even though it happens to nearly everyone."

"That is insane," Amartanon protested.

"It is, in a way," Mara replied. "But they all live on the promise that if they do enough, maybe one day they will become wealthy enough to avoid this. It almost never happens. But because it does happen on rare occasions, they all keep doing hoping it will happen to them. Such is their lives."

"So some escape from this?"

"Yes, but even they are not happy. They are alone in a world of opulence. What good is having many shiny things when you stepped on everyone in order to get them? You see, the wealth they acquire serves only themselves. Thus they are as alone as the poor souls warehoused here."

"Can't we tell them that all of this leads to nothing?" Amartanon asked.

"You can tell them, but they will not believe you. They won't even hear you. The lie has been drilled into their heads since birth, and they are now a slave to it. Each of them believes that there is a reward waiting somewhere in the future. They live so fully for that future that their entire lives pass them by such that they never truly live at all. They exist, nothing more."

"Surely they must take breaks from time to time," Amartanon replied. "Don't they take vacations or something?"

They do," Mara answered, "But their vacations too are rigidly scheduled by the demands of the clock. You see, they know nothing but the clock. So when they try to 'get away from it all and relax,' they do not realize that they themselves are the very thing they are trying to get away from. They carry their clock with them. They schedule every minute of every day and they are hurried even when they are supposed to be on vacation, supposed to be away from the demands of the clock. These people never relax. They hurry through life and then wonder where their life has gone. But don't trouble yourself. It's late. Let us find a place to sleep for the night."

The two found a spot beside the path in which to lie down and sleep; but Amartanon found his sleep was disturbed. The light, the noise and all of the activity moving about prevented him from falling into the blissful silence needed for proper rest. The energy of the place was the energy of need, the energy of want, the energy of "must do." It permeated everything; it even permeated sleep such that rest was not rest, it was a mere pause in the activity— and a pause was no respite, for when paused, the next thing that must be done is waiting to be done such that the longer the pause, the greater the anxiety. Rest was something forever around the next corner, forever waiting, promising to come after the next thing to do is done. It was always in the future, never in the now. Amartanon tried to sleep, but the energy of the village troubled

47

him. He felt it all around him like some dirty film that he longed to wash away. Amartanon eventually fell into a fitful sleep. The energy permeating the village punctured the veil of his dreams and visions appeared in the eyes of his mind.

He saw himself in the dream, and with him was Mara. He saw people standing in a line, waiting to enter a dilapidated shack. Each one entered the shack, and when they came out again, they had a large heavy cross strapped to their backs which they carried about. Amartanon stared off into the valley, and everywhere he looked he saw people laboring under the strain of their crosses. Some were proud of their cross and showed it off to each person they met, proclaiming things like, "Look at how heavy and burdensome this cross is that I am carrying," as if the heavier the cross, the more value they had as a person, but most carried their crosses blissfully unaware that they were doing so. If for any reason one of them should lose their cross, they immediately ran back to the line and got themselves another.

"What is this madness?" he asked Mara in his dream.

"It certainly does seem like madness," Mara replied.

"Why do they do this? Why are they burdening themselves so?'

"They have been taught this behavior," Mara answered. "They have done this their entire lives. They add this unnecessary burden to their lives because they have been taught that this is what life is. Some are very proud of their crosses, and they brag to one another about how difficult their cross is to bear. But most carry theirs out of habit, and they aren't aware they are doing it. Even those who show-off about the crosses they know about are carrying other, larger crosses that they do not realize they have. It is the way with these people."

"That is the most foolish thing I've ever seen," Amartanon replied.

"I would not be so quick to judge them," Mara said. "It is often far easier to see the cross of another than it is to see your own."

"What is that supposed to mean?" Amartanon asked.

"Look at your own back and see."

He turned, and to his horror he found that he too carried a cross—a cross that, before that very moment, he was blissfully unaware existed.

"But... how?" he exclaimed.

"It is the way of all people," Mara answered. "But once you see your cross, you can choose to let it go, to no longer be burdened with it."

"I can let it go?" he asked.

"You need only drop it," Mara answered.

It was then that a strange sensation came over Amartanon. He felt the full weight of the cross, he felt the overwhelming burden of carrying it with him, but for some unknown reason he did not want to let it go. He had carried it for so long that it seemed to have grown into him—to have become a part of him. His eyes locked onto Mara's, pleading. He wanted to let it go, but he could not. There was an unknown force acting within him, a force that acted outside of his control. And that force commanded Amartanon to hold on to his cross. It feared losing the cross for it knew not who it was without it.

Mara, sensing this, spoke. "A man sometimes identifies so completely with his suffering that he becomes nothing but that suffering. To such a man, letting go of suffering is the same as death. He fears letting it go with the same intensity that he fears death. And yet, only by letting it go can he free himself *from* death."

Amartanon struggled to drop his cross, but as he looked upon it, he saw his hand melting into it. Soon there was no hand, just the end of his arm grown into the cross. The wood of the cross began creeping up his arm and his terror grew. He screamed as he felt himself dissolving into wood. It was terrible, painful, and panic surged through his veins like acid searing his flesh from within. He stared at Mara, his eyes pleading for Mara to help him, to save him. But then Mara dissolved into a black nothingness… a void from which nothing could ever escape. It was into that void that Amartanon felt himself drawn. He was to become that nothingness…empty…black, an eternal blank that devoured all he ever was, all he ever hoped to be—everything. It devoured him until it was as if he never was. Dread filled his soul. He gasped, and with that gasp, he startled himself awake.

He panted as he gathered his wits about him. He saw Mara beside the small fire he had made. For a moment Amartanon was not sure if he was awake or if he was still dreaming. He stared at Mara's face, the flickering light casting shadows across it. He noticed Mara smiling, smiling as if he already knew what Amartanon had been dreaming. He rubbed his eyes and sat up.

"I had a bad dream," Amartanon said.

Mara nodded. He leaned toward Amartanon and spoke in a quiet, kindly yet stern voice. "The dream is reality to the person who is dreaming," he said. "In our dreams we tell ourselves the things we need to know, just as in our lives we give ourselves the things we need to experience."

Amartanon stared at Mara, speechless.

"You saw the cross?" Mara asked.

"Yes. How did you know?"

Mara smiled. "I know many things," he said. "I know far more than you think I know. For example, I know that people acquire crosses out of necessity. They go through a difficult time in life, and they convert whatever it was they did to survive, to get through it, into a cross. As such, those crosses in many ways saved the lives of the people who now carry them. They therefore believe they need the cross always. They do not know that once it has served its purpose, it is best to let it go."

"I don't understand, Mara," Amartanon protested. His body quivered with fear; beads of sweat collected on his forehead.

Mara picked up a stick and began poking the fire.

"It is said that we all have our cross to bear," Mara said. "But no one seems to ask why. Why do we have crosses to bear? And is that statement even true? Why bear them at all? I mean, if you really think about it, why pick one up in the first place?"

"Sometimes things happen in life," Amartanon said.

"Yes, they do," Mara answered. "But that does not mean we must forever carry some great suffering on our backs. We add that to the experience. We could instead just experience whatever it is, learn from it, and let it go—completely."

"How does one do that?"

"I suppose you would have to stop the dialog, the chatter in your mind. It's like we have a tiny man in our head describing play by play the events of our life. He is the one who tells us how unfair this was, or how wrong that was. If he would simply shut up, we would all be much happier."

"He never shuts up," Amartanon replied sheepishly, and he smiled a knowing smile, his fear now subsiding.

Mara smiled too and laid down beside the fire. The conversation ended as the two drifted off to sleep.

Amartanon woke the following morning feeling tired and listless, not rested. Fitful dreams continued to plague him through the night. Even the cat seemed troubled by the energy of this place. Amartanon stood to shake off the feeling of anxiety now penetrating his being, and decided it was time to leave this village. It was evident that no one here wanted to hear what Amartanon had come to say.

As they headed along their way, they came upon a small path leading away from the village, and they noticed that many of the busy villagers left their busy doings to walk down this particular path.

"What do you suppose *they* are doing?" Amartanon asked.

"I'm not certain," Mara answered. "Perhaps we should follow them and see."

The two followed this path, along with the occasional villager taking time away from his or her busy work. They soon came upon a tall building made of stone. The building seemed as if it was a *part of* the village though it stood alone, *apart from* the village.

"These stones are very old," Amartanon said examining the stones from which the building was constructed. "They appear tired and worn."

"They are old indeed," Mara replied. "They seem as though they might crumble at any moment bringing the entire edifice down on the heads of those inside."

Amartanon stared at the tall steeple atop the building and noticed it was leaning ever so slightly to one side. He wanted to follow the villagers inside so as to see what they were doing, but he feared it might not be safe. Mara, noticing Amartanon's concern, spoke.

"It hasn't fallen yet," he said. "I think it will be okay to go in."

The two walked up the stone steps which were slippery with moss and dew. They had to walk carefully, deliberately so as to avoid slipping. They made their way to the two large oak doors and pushed them open. The doors creaked loudly. Amartanon felt a foreboding just at the periphery of his awareness. It hovered in that part of the psyche that is but is not. It is that place where the thing is felt but not known. He felt himself unsure, as if what awaited him inside was something unclean—impure. He swallowed hard to still his fear, and the two did enter.

Inside, the building was beautiful to behold. The stones were carefully polished, and there was no sign of the decay the two had seen outside. The doors opened to a vast room with ceilings reaching high above their heads. Sunlight shone through beautiful stained glass, casting a colorful and subdued glow throughout. The people inside spoke with a reverent softness. There were pews in carefully placed lines facing an altar. A priest stood at the altar speaking incantations as villagers either sat in the pews listening with their eyes closed, or knelt in deep prayer. Another priest who had been carefully watching the two since they entered approached them and motioned them to follow him to a small room off to one side away from the others.

"You are new here?" the priest asked.

"Yes," Amartanon answered.

"We are so very pleased to see you," the priest continued. His gaze then shifted to Mara and he scowled his recognition. "What is *he* doing here?" the priest asked in disgust. He turned his back to Mara in an intentional act of disrespect, and continued speaking with Amartanon acting as if Mara was not there. He cleared his throat and smiled a crooked smile to Amartanon. "We seldom receive visitors anymore," he said.

Amartanon stood perplexed. He didn't understand why the villagers, who while in the village seemed too busy to take even a few moments to speak, would come here and do what appeared to be nothing but sit in silence.

"What do you do here?" he asked.

"Oh," the priest replied, "We do wonderful things here. We are the keepers of the gift."

"And what gift might that be?"

"It is the gift of eternal peace. It is the gift of God."

Amartanon tilted his head. "You give them this gift?" he asked.

"We do," the priest replied. "We remind them of how much God loves them and of how proud God is of the many things they do down in the village."

"I do not understand," Amartanon replied. "What need have they of you for this?"

"Oh, they are so very busy that they do not have much time to sit and reflect, and they often forget," the priest answered. "We remind them that if they keep doing all of those important things that they do, God has a special place for them after they die where they will be able to rest, and they will at long last receive great rewards."

"Are they happy doing all the things they do in the village?"

"That is not relevant," the priest replied. "Happiness comes to those who are obedient, and God rewards their obedience with wonderful luxuries in heaven, at least he does this for those who are saved."

"Saved from what?" Amartanon asked.

"You know, saved from the sin they were born into," the priest answered.

Amartanon stared inquisitively at the priest. "So they are born broken? They live their lives doing because to do is what was always done? They are tired and unhappy now, but they do all of this so they can be happy after they are dead?"

"Why yes," the priest replied, "That is the way. It is the mystery of God."

Amartanon shook his head in disbelief. "I do not understand," he said. "Can't they be happy now *and* go to heaven after they die?"

"That is theoretically possible," the priest answered. "But the things that must be done are often, shall we say, mundane. However, this is itself a part of the wonder of obedience to God. To keep doing the mundane things that must be done requires great faith, and that faith manifests as obedience. So they do these things to demonstrate their obedience, and for this they will receive the greatest of rewards in heaven."

"And what if you are wrong?"

"What do you mean?" the priest asked.

"What if they don't go to this heaven you speak of after they die? Then they will have given up that which they now have for that which never was and will never be. It would seem to me a far better thing to be happy now, to make the most out of what you know you have, rather than to trade it all away for a promise of that which may never be."

The priest frowned at these words. Such questions made him uncomfortable.

"What is so important about these things that they do?" Amartanon asked.

"They do that which must be done," the priest snapped. "But you ask too many questions. Don't question what we do. God doesn't like it when we ask too many questions because he wants us to have faith in him and do his bidding. Here, take this and you will feel better; you will become calm, and you will feel the presence of God inside of you." The priest extended his hand, and upon it was a rancid little wafer. "Go on, take it," he insisted. "It is the flesh of God." His eyes narrowed into a wicked gleam behind his crooked smile.

"What does this do?" Amartanon asked.

"It does for you what you cannot do for yourself," the priest answered.

Amartanon glanced over to Mara who stood silently watching. He turned back to the priest. "This looks like poison," he said.

"Oh, that's ridiculous," the priest replied. "After all, the scientists in the village have assured us that it is perfectly safe. This will not harm you; as I said before it will calm you and make you feel the presence of God. This is the flesh of God, and we are the keepers of it. The wafer will make you feel at peace as you go about doing the many important things that must be done. Its effects will last a couple of days, then you must come back so that we might give you another. We do, of course, request that you pay a small fee in the form of a donation. But this first one is free. Go on. Try it!"

Amartanon stared at the wafer—wretched little thing it was. He then stared hard into the priest, the keeper of God. His vision began to shift as the outward appearance of the priest faded from view and the inward reality of the man made itself known to him. The beauty of the priest disappeared, and what stood before him was a troll—the embodiment of the decrepitude of the one who would sell salvation. His body was as wretched as the outside of the church. Where the outside of the church was in shambles, but the inside appeared polished and beautiful; the outside of the priest was polished but what was in him was rotten to the core. Amartanon spat on the poisoned wafer being offered him, and the ugliness of the priest immediately burst through.

"Infidels!" the priest shouted. "I banish you from this place! I banish you to an eternity of torment after you die!" The priest swung the door of the small room open, shoved the two into the larger enclosure, and shouted for all those in the church to hear. "Here are two who deny God!" he wailed. "Look upon this man. He brings his devil with him into this house of worship. We must band together against him, for he is the darkness. He is that which you all fear."

The people turned to look upon Amartanon and his devil, scorn painted upon their faces.

Amartanon shouted in reply. "You people have been sold a lie," he protested. "You have no need of this place to give to you that which is already within you. Stop partaking of this poison."

But the stones heard him better than did the people. The conditioning of their minds taught them how not to hear that which was not supposed to be spoken; whereas stones do not have minds, therefore they hear everything. But even stones grow tired and weary, and the weight of this place was nearly more than the stones could bear. Amartanon rushed out of the building with Mara following behind, the priest shouting curses after them. Amartanon spoke.

"This building will one day fall upon them, Mara," he said. "It cannot stand but so long. Even stones cannot be forced to forever defy that which is." Mara nodded and the two set off on their way, the cat trailing along behind them.

CHAPTER 5

They wandered down the path past the village and into the countryside. The sun shone down forcefully upon them. The air, heavy with moisture, made breathing a chore. They had not walked long when they stumbled upon an old man sitting beside the path, his hair grey, his skin wrinkled. He seemed lost in thought, distracted.

"Hello, good sir," Amartanon said as he and Mara approached.

The old man sitting beside the path looked up startled. He had not noticed them approaching so lost was he in his thoughts.

"Who are you?" the old man asked.

"I am Amartanon and this is my companion Mara. We are on a journey to explore this valley and bring the message from the mountain to the people here," Amartanon answered.

The old man stared at the two quizzically. "*You* have a message to bring?" he asked. "I am the teacher here. I have a message for you."

"You have a message for us?" Amartanon asked. "And what might that be?"

"That there is no need to travel to find answers," the old man said. "All the answers people seek can be found by thinking."

"By thinking?" Amartanon asked. "How can that be so?"

"You must understand," the old man replied, "That the things of this world are nothing but imperfect manifestations of the perfect. It is the idea that is most real, not the particular thing. As such, one need only pontificate to find, for it is in the mind and only in the mind that the perfect form exists. One does not learn, so much as one remembers that which is now, and has always been, in his mind."

"I do not understand," Amartanon replied with a puzzled look on his face.

"I will teach you," the old man said, "For that is what I do. Now, listen very carefully. I want you to think of something, let us say a horse. I want you to imagine that horse as the perfect example of a horse. It is perfect in every way. Can you do that?"

Intrigued, Amartanon closed his eyes and he did begin to imagine the horse. He saw in his mind's eye the perfect beast, strong and beautiful, yet responsive to his every command. It was indeed the perfect horse.

"Now that you see this image in your mind, can you find such a perfect specimen anywhere in what you refer to as this real world?"

SOPHOS

"I have seen similar such animals," Amartanon replied.

"Yes, but if you think about it, all of them fall short in some way of this image you have in your mind, do they not?"

Amartanon thought about this. "I suppose that is true," he said.

"No such animal as the one you are imagining can exist in this world, correct?"

"I would have to agree," he replied.

"But the fact that you can imagine it means that it must actually be; it must actually exist, for if it did not, you could not imagine it. You cannot imagine anything that does not exist somewhere, correct?"

"I think I can," Amartanon protested.

"Then do it for me," the old man continued. "Imagine for me right now something that does not exist. Now be careful here, you must imagine something that never existed. This means you cannot put together things that do exist and from that create something that never was, such as a lion with wings. No part of what you are to imagine can ever have existed in any reality. You must build something completely new without any part of it ever having existed anywhere. Can you do it?"

Amartanon thought for a moment, but everything he tried to imagine was built upon a memory of something he knew to exist already. He found it impossible to create something in his mind of which he was not already aware. "It seems," he said, "That I cannot imagine something completely new. It has to have some existence somewhere, and I have to have some experience of it before I can imagine it at all."

"That is precisely my point," the old man said. "Unless it first exists, your mind cannot know it."

"I don't understand. Tell me again, your point is?" Amartanon asked.

"The point is that the perfect horse must exist somewhere or you would not be able to imagine such a thing," the man said. "This is why the perfect must exist somewhere, but the images of the perfect manifesting in this reality are flawed. They are but an approximation of the original perfect idea. Therefore, to know a thing, you must think of it, not as it appears here in this earthly plane, but as it exists in perfection as an *idea*. All of this around us is but a reflection of that sublime concept. The ultimately real is the idea, not the thing."

Amartanon thought about this, and he found the argument compelling; yet something did not sit well within him. He stared at Mara who said nothing. Mara simply smiled and listened to the conversation unfolding. Amartanon pondered. He struggled to find the flaw in the argument, but he could not find it even though he felt it to exist.

"There is something missing here," he said. "Your logic seems flawless, yet something about it is not right."

The old man replied, "This is because you are enamored with the shadows of the ideas. You are blinded by the image of the thing and cannot see through to the idea itself. The idea is the perfect thing, unfettered by the material image it projects."

And with those words the thought came to him. "You speak of perfect," he said. "That is the flaw in your argument. That is the thing that can be thought that does not exist. Perfect is nothing but a human judgment imposed upon the real. What *you* see as perfect is not the same as what *I* see as perfect. There is no perfect; there is only that which is. You, old man, sit in judgment of the world and because of this you have condemned it. Worse than that, you have denied it its reality because it somehow fails to live up to that which you think it should be. For your words to be true, someone's idea of perfect would have to be accepted as the true perfect. As everyone's judgment is different, there can be no consensus on that. I might see a docile horse as perfect; whereas you may see fire and wildness in him as perfect. The world you speak of exists nowhere but in your mind. You have denied that which is, in favor of your idea of what should be. This makes you the denier of all that is real."

The old man stared hard into Amartanon's eyes, and with a dismissive wave of his hand, closed his mind to the words spoken to him. This was, after all, a less than perfect man speaking utter nonsense.

"The idea alone is real," the old man protested, "any thinking person would know that. Everything else is nothing."

"But that seems to be the problem," Amartanon replied. "You are thinking. Thinking has its uses, but it is no substitute for the actual experience, the real thing. Thinking is a wonderful servant, but a terrible master. You should lord over the thought and yet you let the thought lord over you."

The old man stared back at Amartanon. "You, my dear boy, are simply of a lesser mind and as such you cannot see. Be on your way now." The old man waved the two away as if shooing a fly.

Amartanon wanted to say something, but he saw the futility of speaking further to the old man beside the path. The old man had never travelled the path; he merely sat beside it and imagined the journey. Nothing in him was of any value, for he was himself nothing but an idea. He could not see that this imperfect image that he thought himself to be would itself be quite incapable of imagining that which was perfect. His own musings contained within them the seeds of their own failure. The imperfect thinking within his imperfect mind thought itself to be perfect. The old man knew nothing for he did nothing, and Amartanon knew that everything that can be known must be known through doing. To know through words or thought only is but an abstraction, and as such it is one step removed from that which is real. It is the experience, not the idea, that matters.

The two left the old man beside the path and walked for some time in silence. "Mara," Amartanon at long last spoke, "That was a most unusual man."

"In what way?" Mara asked.

"He does not seem to value the material world. He has no idea that 'matter' is the 'mater,' or 'mother,' of all that is."

"And what do you think?" Mara asked.

"I think the spirit is the father, the material is the mother, and it is through the mother that the father expresses. I think they depend one upon the other. Neither is primary. Neither is better than the other. Neither supersedes the other. They simply dance."

"Interesting thought," Mara replied. "Coming as it does from he who violated Sophia so that he might enter this valley."

Amartanon paused to consider these words. Sophia's face flashed in his mind. He saw her lying on the ground weeping having just suffered his abuse. He felt a deep sense of shame and guilt, but no sooner did he feel it than he quickly pushed it away; he would not let his mind know of it. He instead sought refuge in his pride and found rationalizations to justify the inexcusable.

"Is that not the way?" he asked. "Isn't the violation necessary if this journey is to happen? I can see no other way."

"I suppose that is true of *this* journey," Mara replied. "But perhaps not for every journey. I think it depends upon what the traveler is to learn. What do you think you are to learn?"

"I am not here to learn!" Amartanon snapped, his pride now swelling into anger. "I am here to teach."

Mara smiled. "I must be mistaken," he said. "If you are here to teach, then teach you must. But I do sometimes wonder who the student is."

"We shall find him soon enough," Amartanon replied. "I will do that which I came here to do."

With that, the two walked on in silence. It was a beautiful, warm day. They wandered along a crooked path, winding this way and that, the trees swaying gently in the soft breeze, leaves rustling, birds flitting about chirping melodically. The cat seemed to be recovering from her wounds, and she followed the two walking closer to them than before. Time meant little here. In fact, there was no time; only the movement of the sun across the sky. Amartanon decided to speak.

"Your words trouble me, Mara," he said. "But I do not know why."

Mara smiled a knowing smile, compassionate and warm. His smile seemed to comfort Amartanon. "It's getting late," he said. "Let us sit here beside the path and rest. It will be night soon."

Amartanon agreed and the two sat. The cat walked up and lay near him, closer than before. She began licking herself, cleaning her stained and matted fur. Amartanon fetched her some water and tossed her a morsel of food which she ate graciously.

Mara then spoke. "You know," he said. "This valley is of such a nature that I can give you anything you want within it. It will bend to my will in any way that I will it. If there is anything you want, you need only let me know and I can make it be."

Amartanon considered these words. He then considered the idea of the perfect world as he would have Mara make it. This idea appealed to him. He could solve every problem, end all suffering. He needed only to tell Mara how the world *should* be. But as he thought about it in a deeper way, he found himself troubled. "What could I do to improve it?" he thought. And he began to see that the valley was as it was. His view of how to make it better would only result in making it better *for him*. A new understanding came to him. He began to see that, whatever idea he might have of how the world *should* be, was in reality a rejection of the world *as it is*. To give in to that temptation was not only to play God, it was an absolute assertion that God Himself is flawed and that he, a man, knew better than He who created him. He tilted his head and stared deeply into Mara's eyes.

"I cannot bring myself to accept such a proposition, Mara," he said. "To do such a thing would be a condemnation of all that is. I cannot even begin to imagine what I could do to make that which is better than it is. Who am I to say that what is, is not exactly as it should be?"

Mara smiled his agreement. "You have grown wise, my traveler. Perhaps there is hope for you after all."

"I do not understand the words you speak, Mara," Amartanon replied. "You tempt me, then you seem pleased that I reject that which you offer. What kind of devil are you?"

"I am the only kind of devil there ever was," Mara replied.

The sun set below the horizon. The sky grew still and dark. In the distance thunder softly rumbled. "It seems there is a storm brewing," Mara said. "We must get some sleep. Somehow I feel we will need our rest."

Amartanon agreed and found himself a soft spot in the grass upon which to lie down. The cat walked over to lie beside him. He reached to pet the animal, but she hissed yet again and refused to be touched. Amartanon smiled at the animal for, though he was not consciously aware of it yet, he had grown to love her. His mind grew still, and soon he drifted off to sleep.

CHAPTER 6

Amartanon awoke to the cool morning air gently caressing his face. Dew gathered on the blades of grass and the sky was crystal clear and vibrantly blue. The storm that threatened the night before passed and was now a distant memory. The cat walked to Amartanon and rubbed against his leg, purring. Amartanon smiled at the creature. He reached down to pet her, but she hunched her back and once again hissed her disapproval.

"She may never come to love you," Mara said.

Amartanon glanced up at Mara as he considered these words. "That doesn't matter," he said. "I will love her and that will be enough."

Amartanon tossed a few morsels of food toward the cat and she ate them. Her stained fur appeared whiter now. The cat's strength was returning. "This is a good thing," Amartanon thought, and as he thought, he realized that which he felt the night before outside of awareness—that he loved the cat. This gave him pause as he had just said to Mara that he would love the cat, and even though he said the words, he was not yet aware of the feeling growing within him. Now his love came fully into the light of awareness and he felt it intensely. "Strange," he thought, "that I can feel a thing before I know I am feeling it." He then thought that the cat also loved him, albeit in the reserved and fearful way that was the only way in which she could.

When the cat finished eating, Amartanon and Mara stood and resumed their walk in silent contemplation, for there was nothing at the moment to be said. They simply basked in the beauty of the valley as they travelled along. It was a most peaceful sojourn, dream-like, pleasant.

A beautiful meadow opened into a valley before them, fragrant white flowers blossoming as far as the eye could see. Amartanon gazed with wonder at the beauty of this place. He saw bees buzzing about busily gathering nectar from the many white flowers. In the center of the meadow he saw three hills jutting up out of the valley, and he saw in the distance three men standing, one atop each of the three hills. Each of the men had before him a full length mirror into which he continually gazed.

"That is a most strange and unusual sight," Amartanon said to Mara. "I wonder what those men are doing."

"Let us approach them and see," Mara replied.

They wandered through the meadow in the valley and approached the first man on the first hill. They noticed that, though the man appeared vile and wicked, his reflection in the mirror was radiant and beautiful. The vile man noticed them approaching, and he turned from admiring himself to address his visitors.

"Why have you come here?" he asked, his eyes narrowing suspiciously in an attempt to discern the motives of the two strangers.

"We are on a journey," Amartanon replied, Mara smiling beside him. "We came upon this valley and this beautiful meadow sitting within it, and we noticed you standing on this hill. We thought this a curious thing, so we came to inquire as to why you are standing here?"

"I have a message for all who come this way," the vile looking man answered.

"Really," Amartanon replied surprised. "And what might that message be?"

"I am here to proclaim the will of God," said the vile looking man. He pointed to the book he held in his hand, tapping it with his crooked finger. "It is written here that God is pure and wonderful and He is everything good and beautiful," he continued. "We are all, each one of us, to surrender to God and do His bidding. He is such a wonderful and loving God."

"And who exactly is this God?" Amartanon asked.

"Why, He is the one and only God. He commands us to live by every word in this book; and He will smite all of those who fail to do so." He held the book high, waving it above his head. "An eternity of agony awaits those who deny Him. Will you surrender to His will, my friend?"

Amartanon pondered this request. He looked at the reflection of the man in the mirror and was stunned by the radiant beauty reflected there. Then he stared at the man standing before him and found himself so repulsed by the man's ugliness that he did not know how to reconcile the two.

"I must ask," Amartanon replied, "If your God is so loving, why is he so cruel that he, as you have suggested, would inflict an eternity of agony upon those you say he loves?"

"God hates those who would deny him," the vile man answered.

"Yours is a God of hate?"

"He only hates those who sin and act in opposition to his commands," the vile man answered. "He wants us to love Him and to worship Him. He gets angry with us when we refuse to live according to His will. We are all born into sin, and God wants us to beg His forgiveness for that sin. When we follow His will, our lives become beautiful. You can look upon me and see what I have become since I chose to follow Him." The man said this while staring at himself in the mirror, admiring a reflection that hid from the man the truth of himself. "God will save you from the sin you were born into," he continued. "He will rescue you from your suffering."

Amartanon thought about this. He felt a strange allure toward the idea that he could be saved from the evil that was apparently instilled in him. For he knew himself well; and he knew that he could be a better man than he was. Here before him stood a man who promised that this could be done for him. He need only allow this man's God to do it. It would require no effort on Amartanon's part. As strong as that allure proved to be, he could not ignore the fact that the reflection in the mirror did not reflect the real man at all. It seemed to him that an image of beauty was no beauty at all. It was nothing but an illusion; a play of light upon the silvered glass.

Amartanon thus inquired. "You say your God is the God who created me. Is that correct?"

"He is," the vile man replied. "He created you and me and everything in the universe."

"If that is true, then I must reject your God," Amartanon replied. "For you have presented me with a God who hates me as he created me, and wishes instead to force me to be other than what he created. He asks that I beg his forgiveness for being born into the sin he bore me into. If I am such a sinful creature, would not the sin of He who created me be a far worse sin than mine? No sir! Your God is no God at all. He is nothing but a lesser God wanting to be the true God and needing me to play along with his illusion so that I might convince him that he is the supreme God. I must respectfully reject that notion. For if the infinite wonder that is God needs my approval to convince him that he is God, then he is no God at all."

The vile man scowled. He then turned to Mara. "You are the Devil!" he shouted. "You have corrupted this man's thinking, and because of you he denies his God."

He then turned to Amartanon and shouted, "You are the blasphemer! Be gone from me and take your devil with you! You and your demon will most assuredly burn in hell, for that is what you deserve."

Amartanon happened to glance in the mirror as the vile man shouted, and he saw, for the briefest moment, that the mirror reflected him as he truly was. He caught a glimpse in which even the mirror betrayed the truth of the vile man. But when the vile man turned from them to face the mirror himself, the radiant beauty that this man believed himself to be returned, and all was well in the vile man's reality. Mara and Amartanon turned and walked away, the vile man shouting obscenities behind them.

"Are you my Devil?" Amartanon asked, perplexed.

"I do not know," Mara replied. "Am I?"

"It would seem that everyone here thinks so." He paused to consider his next words. "I am troubled, Mara," he continued. "I did not ask you to journey with me. Sophia insisted upon it. And now you seem attached to me and I cannot escape you. I wonder if the people here are correct. Perhaps I *am* influenced by a Devil."

"That is a decision you will have to make for yourself," Mara replied.

"You see! That…right there! Are these words designed to confuse me? Seriously, that is a decision 'I' will have to make? You speak as if you are whatever I decide you are; as if what you are will change according to my whim."

Mara stared at him and said, "Confusion serves its purpose."

Amartanon's anger surged. "You're doing it again. Are you intentionally trying to keep me twisting, turning in the wind? Tell me what you are. If you are a devil, say so. If not tell me that."

Mara smiled. "If I were a devil, would I not lie and say that I am not? Like it or not, this is not something for me to claim; it is

73

something for you to decide. I am not trying to confuse you. You are confusing yourself. There is much you do not see; much you do not know. I only say to you whatever it is that needs to be said. I know that my words *seem* confusing at times. But this is not a function of my words. It is instead a function of your thinking. When *your* mind clears, *my* words will make perfect sense."

Amartanon sighed a heavy, exasperated sigh as he thought about this. He no longer knew what to believe. The people in the valley seemed to despise Mara, and they blamed Mara for the fact that Amartanon challenged their beliefs, as if they could not imagine a person disagreeing with them therefore they thought it had to be the work of a devil. But Mara did not influence Amartanon's disagreement with these people. Amartanon did that on his own. He felt a deep disturbance but did not quite know why. He could not find the words to express what he was feeling.

"Don't think so hard, my friend. The answers will come to you in time," Mara reassured him. Then Mara spoke no more, leaving Amartanon troubled and in doubt.

The two made their way to the second man on the second hill. This man was sitting cross legged, meditating, a cat-o-nine tails in his right hand with which he flogged himself repeatedly. The man sat, emaciated, his ribs protruding through leathery skin. Amartanon wondered how long this poor soul had gone without food. He appeared weak and frail, his back scarred and bleeding. He feared the man might soon die. Yet as they looked into the mirror before this man, they saw reflected there a man of perfect health, radiant, and in a state of sublime peace and serenity.

"What are you doing to yourself?" Amartanon protested. "What is this madness?"

The emaciated man opened his eyes and with a weak voice that was little more than a strained whisper, spoke.

"Life is suffering," he said. "We must learn to endure suffering if we are to find peace. Toward that end I set out on the life of the ascetic. I have embraced suffering so that I might better accept the suffering that is all of life. I eat but three grains of rice a day. My body cries out with the agony of constant hunger. I endure this. I flog my back all day, every day. My body cries out begging mercy and relief from the torment. I ignore this. Thus, I have embraced suffering fully. Because life is suffering, and I embrace suffering, I therefore embrace life. You can see…" the man continued as he pointed to his reflection in the mirror, his arm so weak he strained to lift his hand, "that I have achieved a state of perfect peace."

Amartanon pondered what he was hearing, and again the argument presented him made sense. Life *is* suffering. Surely learning to endure suffering would lead to a sense of peace. After all, there is nothing one can do to prevent suffering, so why not accept it fully? Yet, as he thought deeper, an awareness took hold in his mind. With this realization, he spoke.

"I agree with you," he said, "that life is filled with suffering. But life is not *all* suffering. In fact, there is as much pleasure in life as there is suffering. You cannot have the one without the other.

Is it not true that you are enduring this agony because of the pleasure you believe it to be bringing you? Are you not exactly like everyone else, doing that which you believe will bring you the greatest pleasure? You are wasting away; you are nearly dead. What good is this pleasure you seek if it kills you to find it? You say you are embracing life? I do not see that as so. To me, you are denying life. You are the antithesis of life. You are denying all pleasure in the name of pleasure—though you refer to your pleasure as the 'embracing of suffering.' This makes no sense to me."

The ascetic smiled. "The proof is in the mirror," he said. "You can see that I have achieved a state of perfect bliss. You may go on with the suffering of your life. Leave me to the suffering of mine."

Amartanon and Mara turned and left the ascetic to the death that they were certain was only a short time away.

As they descended down the hill, Amartanon stopped suddenly, exasperated. He turned to Mara. "Is everyone in this valley insane?" he asked. "They seem backwards, upside down, confused. They seek what they seek in denial of that which they seek. Not a single one knows himself. They see only that which they wish to see reflected in the mirror."

"That is the human condition," Mara replied. "But people do not need a mirror to see what they wish to see in defiance of that which is."

As they approached the third man on the third hill, they heard him shouting as if he were addressing a large multitude of people, though no one was there.

"I am the übermench," he shouted. "I am the overman, the next man. I am the evolution of all men made manifest here and now. I am what all men will one day be."

As they approached, they noticed that this was the tiniest of men. He stood no more than four feet tall. He appeared very weak and very frail, but he strutted about as if he were all-powerful, grand even. The reflection in the mirror before him was that of a regal man standing over six feet tall, beautiful to behold, bold and majestic.

"I see you have spoken to the others in this valley," he said. "Did you notice how misguided they are? The first is beholden to a tiny God. I have no need of Gods. I have evolved beyond them. I claim what I am—state it emphatically with no remorse or doubt. The first man you spoke to sees himself as nothing more than a sheep among sheep, blindly following a God that he and others like him created. He is no man at all. Does he not know that God is dead? That God never was? Has he not the courage to stand as a man and assert his existence because he knows himself to be? He is but a puny follower of Apollo, shackled by what he believes to be his God-given duty. I say he is a fraud. He does not realize that Gods were created by man for man. I no longer have need of them. He is timid and weak, and he has not dared to evolve as I have dared."

The tiny man strutted forth and continued. "You then spoke to that other poor slob who thinks life is nothing but pain and torment. He is a fool. If one must have Gods, then I say Dionysus is the way; not Apollo. Drink heartily of the wine of life, for life is all there is. Nothing exists but that which we see. Gods do not exist, and it is folly to surrender oneself to them. Life is here for us to take, to command, to will ourselves to lord over it. I claim all power for I am Man and as such there is nothing—not even a God—to stop me."

The two stood staring at the frail little man who appeared large and grand in his mirror. Amartanon was struck to the core with the realization that this little man too had an argument that carried a certain appeal. In fact, each man posed an argument that made perfectly logical sense in a strange way. Here was yet another compelling argument. Perhaps it *is* best for man to shed all concepts of Gods and rise above such foolish thinking. There was a strong allure to this argument; but like the others, this argument too did not seem quite right.

Amartanon then spoke. "I hear you, my friend, and your argument is indeed compelling. But you say nothing exists but that which we can see. By that I take you to mean not only through sight, but that which we can hear, taste, smell and feel as well. Therefore nothing exists but that which our senses tell us exists. How am I to know this to be true? I cannot possibly know this to be true; therefore I must take it as an article of faith. This means that your entire philosophy is predicated on faith, on the belief in something that cannot be known absolutely, thus you choose to believe it without any evidence to support it. Is this not the very act that you condemn in others? Are you not, at your core, proclaiming a truth predicated on faith? Are you not stating that it exists *because* of your statement that it exists? This is nothing but words arranged so as to act in blind faith while denying the very faith you are acting from.

"Furthermore, while I agree with you that the other two men on the other two hills are in error, it does not follow that their error makes you correct. While I may not believe in their Gods any more than you, what I see in you is yet another belief in God. You have proclaimed *yourself* as God. As such it is *your* mind that possesses all the power of God. Your mind determines what is real and what is unreal. Your mind is the final arbiter of all. You are a preacher, my friend. You preach a gospel. It is a gospel predicated on the faith in something you cannot know to be true; and it is a gospel proclaiming a God—the God of you."

Suddenly these words penetrated the tiny man, punctured him, deflated him, and the image in the mirror shrank to reflect exactly what he was. The tiny man saw this and spoke feebly, tears forming in his eyes, "There is no God..." And with those words the tiny man retreated into his mind; forever lost to an insanity from which he would never escape. He ran off into the distance shouting at the illusions that now infested his mind.

"You broke him," Mara said.

"I only spoke the truth to him," Amartanon replied.

"You were cruel."

"How was I cruel?"

"The truth is only kind when spoken to those who are ready to hear it. You spoke words he was not ready to hear, and as such, you stole from him his God. It is not an act of kindness to rub reality in a man's face. You must guide him to it; let him discover it on his own."

Amartanon felt badly as he realized the truth of Mara's words.

"Do not fret about it," Mara said. "The deed is done. Learn from it."

The two continued along the path, through the meadow to a forest on the other side. The sun shone high above them. They found a shady place under a tree and sat to rest. The cat seated itself beside Amartanon. Mara looked up and noticed bright red apples growing on the tree under which they sat. He stood to pick one, bit into it, then picked another and handed it to Amartanon sitting beside him. Amartanon too bit into the apple and found it tart yet sweet. He ate the apple absent mindedly, lost in his thoughts such that he was barely aware of his surroundings.

"You appear troubled," Mara said.

"It is those three men," Amartanon answered. "They each have such compelling arguments, and yet each argument is mistaken." He bit again into the apple, savoring its sweetness while trying to ignore the tart taste.

"They are all manifestations of the same thing," Mara said.

"What do you mean?" Amartanon asked. "Each one held opinions that contradicted those of the others."

Perhaps their words were different," Mara replied. "But their words do not matter. They suffer from the same delusion."

"And what delusion is that?" Amartanon asked.

"They suffer from the disease of knowledge," Mara replied.

"I don't understand."

"Each of those men think they know something. In fact, they think they know everything there is to know. Because they know everything, they can learn nothing."

Amartanon pondered this thought for a moment.

Mara continued. "What they think they know is reflected to them in their mirrors. What they *believe* is more real to them than what they are."

"Is there a way to teach them otherwise?" Amartanon asked.

"What can be taught to the man who thinks he knows everything?" Mara asked. "And I am curious, what do you think *you* have to teach them?"

Amartanon thought about this question, but could find no answer.

He struggled to find words that could express what he felt, but as is so often the case, no words were up to the task. At best, the words he might use would only be an approximation. They would never fully describe his feelings; they would instead point in the general direction. The more he struggled the more agitated he became. It felt like a thorn stabbing his brain. At last he answered. "They are mistaken in their views," he said. "It would seem that someone could point that out to them and they could come to see it."

Mara smiled and bit again into the apple. He paused to consider his words, then spoke. "You are correct that they *could* see," he replied. "But they do not *want* to see. It would shatter their world to see anything other than that which they already believe to be true. You witnessed the third man who almost saw, yet he chose insanity over the implications of that which you showed him. They are entrenched in dogma. More than that, they have wrapped their identities in their respective dogmas, as their reflections in the mirrors clearly depict. Do you think for a minute any of those three want to see themselves as they really are? The third one had the courage to look, but it drove him mad. An identity entrenched in dogma becomes as hard as the hardest stone. No chisel on this earth can chip even the tiniest piece from it. Certainly your words would fall on ears unwilling to hear. Men do not want to see themselves as they really are; they want to see themselves as they believe themselves to be. Tell them what they really are and they will do nothing but despise you for it."

"Then what is the point of this journey?" Amartanon protested. "If no one wants to see anything other than what they want to believe, how do I teach them anything?"

"Interesting question," Mara replied. "Perhaps you will have to rethink what it is you believe a teacher to be."

"What do you mean?" Amartanon asked.

"What makes you different from the three men we just encountered? Are you not suffering from the delusion that, because you climbed the mountain, you now know the absolute truth? Are you here to teach? Or did you come here to proselytize? Are you here to help people find their own way? Or do you wish to impose your way upon them? Do you really have anything—anything at all—to teach?"

"But I saw…"

"You saw! You saw! What did you see? It is for each man to see what he is to see. No man is to tell another that which he is *supposed* to see. Your way is nothing but your way. Why must you inflict it upon others?"

Amartanon did not understand this and his heart ached for those he knew to be suffering. He longed to help them, to reach them, but he felt powerless to do anything for them. The cat rubbed up beside him, and he reached down to pet it. This time the cat did not resist, but Amartanon was so lost in his own thoughts that he was unaware of the magic that had just happened.

"I feel I am wasting my time here," he said resignedly, and he let out a heavy sigh.

Mara stared at Amartanon in disbelief. "Will you look at what you are doing right now?" he asked.

Amartanon stared at Mara dumbfounded. "I'm not doing any-thing," he protested.

Mara shook his head. "You want to go out and save all the people in this valley. You feel so badly for those who are suffering, and you feel yourself unable to do anything about it. And yet, you sit before me having done something remarkable, and you don't even see it."

"What?" Amartanon protested. "What have I done? What dif-ference have I made to anyone here?"

"What are you doing with your left hand right now?" Mara asked.

Amartanon stared blankly at Mara and without any thought, answered, "I am petting this..." His words stopped dead.

"Yes," Mara said. "You are petting that cat. It is a cat that came to you hungry and in pain. That cat would not let you near her, and now she is sitting beside you letting you pet her, and you sit there unaware that you are even doing it just as you are unaware of the very real difference your presence has made for that cat. Isn't that the way with you men? When you are blind to that which is evil in you, you are blind to that which is good in you also. Why is it that human beings are forever trying to be one or the other? Why is it so hard to be both?"

Amartanon looked down upon the cat. It was no longer grey and matted. Its fur shone a brilliant white. The cat now expressed the beauty that she was, and it was the care Amartanon had given her that brought this into being.

"Do not for a moment think," Mara continued, his voice softening, "that because it is just a cat, what you did does not matter. What you have done with that poor creature is the purest expression of you. You did not try to force your will upon it. And perhaps most importantly of all, you didn't try to *teach* it anything. You simply loved it and gave it what it needed while asking nothing of it. That cat has learned from you the most valuable of all things. Do you hear what I am saying to you? The cat *learned* a valuable lesson from you because you did not try to *teach*. You simply expressed your love for the animal such that you didn't even notice that you were petting it. *You didn't notice.* That means it simply happened naturally without you trying to force it in any way. Do you get it now?"

Amartanon sat in stunned silence.

"Can't you see, my friend?" Mara asked. "There is so much more than what you know. There is much more to be learned. There is much for *you* to learn. If you are ready to open your heart and open your mind to the possibility that there are many things yet for you to learn, then perhaps we should visit a man I know who may be able to help us. He is a man who has seen more than most. Perhaps he will be able to help you."

Amartanon did not seem to hear Mara, so lost was he in his thoughts. "I no longer know who I am," he said, his voice feeble and weak.

Mara, ignoring this, spoke. "The man I speak of does not live far from here," he said. "Let us visit him and see if he can be of help."

Amartanon, now actually hearing what Mara was saying, looked up at Mara surprised. "You have travelled this valley before?" he asked.

Mara smiled. "Too many times to count."

"But… I thought…"

"Yes, you do have a persistent habit of doing that," Mara interrupted.

"I don't understand…" Amartanon replied.

"That is the most honest thing I have ever heard issue forth from your mouth," Mara said.

Amartanon was about to speak but Mara would not let him. "Drink some of my water," he said as he retrieved a flask from his pocket, "and do not trouble yourself any longer. It cannot be figured out. Your mind will do nothing but confuse you. It is time for you to begin thinking without it. Let us depart from here and visit my friend. He is wise. I think he will have the answers you seek." Mara handed the flask to Amartanon who drank heartily from it for he was parched. He paused to take a breath and then drank more. He paused, then he drank again.

"I seem to have developed an unquenchable thirst," he said.

"It's about time," Mara replied.

"What…"

"Never mind," Mara said. "Let us go now and see my friend.

—

Amartanon took another swig from the flask and handed it back to Mara. He took one last bite from his apple, and tossed the core to the ground. The two then stood and continued on their journey, but now Mara led the way.

CHAPTER 7

It was not long before they came upon a small cottage situated in a clearing in the forest. It was a quaint little place, not much to speak of, but pleasant in its own unassuming way. The two approached the cottage and Mara knocked at the door. They heard the sounds of someone shuffling about inside. Soon the door opened, and there before them stood a man old and weathered, yet he projected a radiance such that one might mistakenly think he was glowing. The old man smiled at Mara and embraced him warmly. He then turned to Amartanon and embraced him as if they had been friends for many years.

"Come in, come in," he said excitedly. "You must sit with me and rest. I have been expecting you."

Amartanon turned to Mara surprised by the words he just heard. He wondered how the old man knew they were coming.

Mara smiled, "Let me introduce to you my friend Solon," he said, gesturing towards the old man.

Solon took Amartanon by the shoulders and stared deeply into him. "So, this is the stone that is beginning to crumble," he said with no further explanation, leaving Amartanon to wonder what he meant by this. He then led the two inside and invited them to sit.

Amartanon was now completely confused and felt more than a bit uncomfortable. Because of this, he said nothing.

"I understand you are a great teacher," Solon said to Amartanon, his eyes bright and eager. "So… Go ahead… Teach me something."

Amartanon felt a surge of indignation, thinking this to be an insult. He also wondered how this Solon knew so much about him when they had never met. Solon, recognizing this, spoke.

"Do not feel badly my friend," he said. "It is not my desire to insult you. I am only attempting to show you something you would rather not consider."

"Mara said *you* might have answers for *me*," Amartanon replied weakly.

"Me?" Solon replied as if shocked by such a thing. "I have nothing to teach. I have no answers to anything."

Amartanon turned to Mara, "I don't understand, Mara," he said. "Why did you bring me here?"

"I thought Solon might have something of value to offer you," he replied.

"But he just said he doesn't."

"I said no such thing," Solon interjected. "I said I have nothing to teach, not that I had nothing to offer. You must be very careful with your words, my friend."

"Teach…offer…what's the difference?" Amartanon asked, his irritation with the man growing.

"There is a world of difference between those two ideas," Solon answered. "To offer is to share my experience. To teach is a different thing entirely. You see, the teacher is in each of us. If I attempt to teach you, I will be denying that there is a teacher in you and I would be assuming that role for myself. That is a most disrespectful and arrogant thing to do to a fellow traveler."

Mara spoke. "He entered the valley because having climbed the mountain he felt he had something to teach the people here. But he is finding the task to be more difficult than he had expected."

"I see," Solon replied.

Amartanon stared at Solon intently. He wanted to dislike this man, but he could not. There was something about him that was likable no matter how irritating he may seem.

"I am not certain he is ready to hear what I have to say," Solon said to Mara, his eyes locked on Amartanon. "But I will say it just the same. Doesn't really matter if he's ready or not, I suppose." Solon then smiled. "Do you want to hear what I have to tell you," he asked.

"Truthfully," Amartanon said, "part of me does, and part of me does not."

"Well then," Solon replied enthusiastically, "we shall speak to the part that does."

Amartanon did not know what to think. He was irritated, but not overly so. His irritation was fast giving way to resignation. He continued to stare hard at Solon, and as he did so, Solon began to appear much younger than he had only a moment before. The radiance that he only caught a glimpse of when they first met now came into clear view. There was an indescribable beauty to this man. Solon's eyes narrowed and he leaned forward to speak.

"My experience has been that until I questioned everything I thought I knew, I was unable to see the world as it really is." Solon spoke in a slow cadence and paused to let his words penetrate Amartanon deeply. "Have you questioned every assumption that exists in you? Have you questioned the deepest assumptions—the ones you have accepted as true though you never considered, not even for a moment, that they might be in error?" he asked.

"I believe I have," Amartanon replied hesitantly.

"Have you allowed yourself to think the forbidden thought?" Solon asked, his eyes gleaming.

This question stirred a deep anxiety in Amartanon, though it was so distant that he was mostly unaware of it. "I do not know," he answered. "I do not know what the forbidden thought might be."

Solon's eyes sparkled and his face grew solemn as he spoke. "There is that deepest of thoughts," he said. "It is a thought so deep and so ingrained that few have ever questioned it. Nearly all people believe it without ever having considered it in what one might call an objective manner. It is simply assumed by all to be true, and as such, we must question it if we are to find what we seek. Tell me that deepest thought—some might even call it the original thought—the one you have never questioned, never even thought to question. What is the core assumption upon which your entire perception of the world is built?"

Amartanon thought about this, and then said, "I suppose it is the idea that I exist."

Solon leaned back in his chair. He turned to Mara, "He is close," Solon said. "But I am not sure if he is yet ready." He then leaned forward looking deep into Amartanon's eyes, and he spoke.

"We will leave the question of existence aside for now," he said. "There is something even more important that we must consider. Your entire world view, whether you know it or not, is based upon a premise. And it is this premise that could be mistaken. It might not be mistaken. Or some of it may be accurate, while other parts are in error. I cannot tell you that it is mistaken. I cannot tell you that it is not. What I can tell you is that we must explore the possibility that it *is* mistaken, and then examine the evidence. If, once we have done that, we find that reality suddenly makes more sense than it had before, we must then abandon the mistaken assumption for the new thought. If we find that abandoning the assumption does not make sense, then we must keep it. The idea is to examine everything, even our most deeply held beliefs. For if there is an error found in the depths of our beliefs, the foundation upon which we have built our perception of reality will also be flawed, and it will never be reconciled. Are you ready to answer the question that you never thought to ask?"

"I suppose I am," Amartanon replied.

"Very well then," Solon said. "I will tell you the thing you have believed—all people believe—at the very core of your being. You have never truly questioned it. You may have had doubts from time to time, but you shoved them from your mind. Here it is..." Solon paused and drew a deep breath. "Your core assumption that you have never questioned is simply this: That God is good and the Devil is bad."

Amartanon stared at Solon, perplexed. "You say everyone has this core belief, and that they haven't questioned it? What about Atheists? Haven't they asked that question? I myself have asked that question as I have seen many bad things done in the name of God."

"You are not looking deeply enough," Solon replied. "At the deepest level of every person raised in this society, there is this idea of Good versus Evil. We begin our lives anthropomorphizing these concepts, turning them into God and Devil. But it is the core assumption of Good and Evil that I am speaking of here."

"So you are using the words God and Devil to represent Good and Evil?" Amartanon asked.

"I am saying that they are the same thing," Solon replied. "I prefer God and Devil because those words are charged with incredible energy in the hearts and minds of people. Even Atheists have their Gods. They appeal to the God of Justice in their attempt to move away from the God of the Bible. They also appeal to other Gods, such as the God of Materialism, or the God of Science, or the God who breathes order into evolution. They call this God by many names, such as energy, or cause and effect. They have an unwavering faith in these Gods, just as many of the devoutly religious have absolute faith in their Gods. But the Theist and the Atheist both act in accordance with the demands of their respective Gods. They both attempt to impose upon the world their idea of what is moral, what is right. I am asking you to go deeper into the very concept of what is good and what is right. How do you know a thing to be good, or another thing to be evil?"

Amartanon thought this to be a strange question. "Everyone knows right from wrong," he said.

"Do they?" Solon asked. "Then tell me, what is right and what is wrong?"

Amartanon shook his head, an indication of how stupid he thought this question to be. But Solon simply stared at him; his stare demanding an answer.

"Anything that harms a person, or causes them pain is evil," he at last answered. "Anything that is helpful to a person and makes them feel better is good."

"I see," Solon answered. "Then let us explore your idea and see if it holds true, shall we?"

Amartanon threw up his hands and shrugged his shoulders as he leaned back in his chair. "This all seems silly," he said in exasperation. "But we're here, so I suppose we can play this silly game of yours."

Solon threw a knowing smile toward Mara. This irritated Amartanon as he felt they were mocking him. Solon seemed to revel in Amartanon's irritation, and this irritated him all the more.

"So, according to your definition of good and bad," Solon said, "let us assume that I take a nasty fall and break my leg. This is a bad thing, yes?"

"I don't know if it is bad, but it is certainly unfortunate."

"Why is it not bad?"

"It was an accident, so there was no intent to break your leg. Had I intentionally broken it, then I would have been doing something bad," Amartanon answered.

"Fair enough," Solon replied. "So we must redefine your original statement to include conscious intent before we can say a thing is an act of good or an act of evil?"

"Yes, I would say that intent is necessary," he answered.

"So an event is morally neutral unless there is some intent behind it," Solon repeated. "If I break my leg, we can say that it is bad, if by bad we mean unfortunate; but we cannot call it bad if by bad we mean an intentional act perpetrated against me. To call it bad in that sense, or evil, we would have to assume there was the intent to cause harm?"

"I suppose that is true," Amartanon answered.

"I am going to suggest then," Solon continued, "that we do not use the word 'bad' because it has many different meanings depending upon the context in which it is used. We shall use the word 'evil' instead. Evil implies intent to harm, does it not?"

"It does."

"Ok then," Solon smiled. "You see, we are already making progress. We have examined your premise, and we found flaws in our use of language that we have corrected." Solon smiled proud of himself.

"So now let us assume that you, quite by accident, bump into me causing me to fall and I break my leg. We might think of this as a bad thing, or unfortunate, but we would certainly not call it an act of evil on your part, correct?"

"That is correct," Amartanon answered. "There would be no intent on my part to harm you."

"Ok then, back to your original definition. You said that anything that harms another person, or causes them pain, is evil; whereas anything that helps them or eases suffering is good?"

"I did."

"We must modify that now to account for what we have discovered. Clearly it is not true that anything that causes harm or pain is evil, because, as in the example before us, if you accidentally cause me to break my leg, no act of evil has occurred. Therefore it is the *intentional* act of inflicting pain or harm upon another that is evil?"

"Yes, that is true."

"Likewise we can say that an act is not good unless there is the intent to alleviate suffering or to help another?"

"I get it," Amartanon said, his voice betraying his irritation. "I forgot to include intent in my definition. I thought that was simply assumed."

"Never assume," Solon reprimanded. "You must be very clear with your use of words, as their meanings are sometimes heard differently by those to whom they are spoken than the meaning you intended when you spoke them. I am not going through this exercise to irritate you. I am doing this so that we can be sure that we are understanding one another."

Solon paused, his eyes locked with Amartanon's signaling his displeasure.

"I understand," Amartanon relented.

Solon continued. "Now, we have determined that an act is evil if it is harmful or if it inflicts pain and it must also carry with it the intent to cause harm, correct?"

"Yes," Amartanon answered.

"Given the necessity of intent," Solon continued, "we can now see that Good and Evil do not exist without human beings."

"I'm not following you," Amartanon replied.

Well, if intent is the prerequisite for an act to be Good or Evil, then the intent comes from a person, does it not?"

"That is not necessarily so," Amartanon argued. "Animals harm one another."

"This is true, but do they do this with the intent to harm? Or do they do this with some other need in mind, such as the drive to eat, or the drive to mate? Does an animal have the ability to decide to inflict harm simply because it wants to be cruel?"

"I suppose not," Amartanon answered.

"It is settled then," Solon continued. "Good and Evil do not exist without human beings to make the act Good or Evil."

"Ok," Amartanon answered. "I see your point."

"It is like what Shakespeare said in Hamlet, 'Nothing is good or bad but thinking makes it so'."

SOPHOS

"I got it," Amartanon said.

"We also say that God is all good, yes?"

"Yes, that is true."

"Since we have determined that good can only come about through an act of human will, surely it must then follow that God is a function of human will. He comes into existence when a human being acts with the intent to do something good. He cannot have any existence outside of that or separate from that. Human beings create God when they perform good deeds."

"Uh…" Amartanon replied, his head reeling. "I'm not sure about that."

"Think about it," Solon replied. Good requires intent to be good. God is good. Therefore God is intent. He is a verb, not a noun."

"You're making sense, but..,"

"I know. It's hard to be logically consistent when logic fails to conform to our expectations, isn't it?" Solon said smiling. "This also wreaks havoc with the Atheist argument that there is no God when every act of good they attempt creates the very God they deny exists."

"But…"

"Oh, but nothing. It's all this personification thing. We made the act of bringing good into this world, or God, something separate from the act itself. We turned God into a man, now we have a hard time recognizing what God really is. But no matter…we should press on."

Amartanon shook his head slowly from side to side, smiling in exasperation.

"Ok, where were we? Oh, yes, my leg was broken. So my leg is now broken, and let us assume it is a bad break so that my leg is no longer straight. Are you with me?"

"Yes," Amartanon replied.

"Now, it would be an act of kindness, and it would be a good thing for you to comfort me, say, help me to bed, bring me food and medication should I require it. These would all be good things?"

"Yes, they would."

"Ok. So according to your definition of what is good, you would comfort me and take care of me in my recovery?"

"This is true."

"Let us then assume that time passes and I get better. You have done nothing but comfort me the entire time, so your actions have been indisputably good?"

"Yes," Amartanon answered.

"But I get out of bed and attempt to walk, only to find that my leg has healed in such a way that it is now forever at an angle and I can no longer walk on it. I needed early on to have my leg put straight so that it would heal in such a way as to allow me to walk again. But to put it straight would have caused me great pain. To accomplish this, you would have been required to inflict incredible pain on me. We have determined that doing so would have been evil as it carried the intent to inflict pain. To comfort me was good, but now I am unable to ever walk again. According to your definition, good sometimes leads to a bad outcome, whereas an act of evil can lead to a good outcome. Am I correct?"

"Well, no, that is not correct. I would certainly need to set your leg so that it would heal properly."

"Ok," Solon replied. "Then we must adjust our definition of Good and Evil yet again. We will now say that sometimes it is good to intentionally inflict pain?"

"Yes, I suppose it is."

"Are you beginning to see?" Solon asked.

"See what?" Amartanon replied.

"That concepts like Good and Evil do not have clear meaning in and of themselves. Their meaning is always relative to the situation *and* relative to the intentions of the person."

"I see what you are saying," Amartanon replied. "So we left out the fact that I must consider what you want as well."

"Then let us consider that now. My leg is broken, and I am in terrible pain. You tell me that you must set it or I may never walk again. But I am in so much pain that the idea of setting my leg is unthinkable to me. I tell you, 'No. You cannot set it.' Now, is it good to simply comfort me? Or is it good to convince me that the leg must be set, and perhaps even force me into having it set should I refuse?"

"I suppose I would have to force you," Amartanon said.

"Can you see now that we can never come to any absolute agreement on Good versus Evil? Our narrow view that we began with was that comforting me was the right thing to do. Now, by stepping back and looking at things in a broader context, we find that inflicting intense pain upon me—and forcing me to submit if necessary—is the ultimate good?"

"That is true," Amartanon replied.

"We have discovered that the concepts of Good and Evil shift according to our perspective. So the question becomes who is the ultimate authority on what is good and what is evil? There is no person who can see every eventuality and every possible outcome. We cannot even use your idea of the intentional infliction of pain as evil, or intentional acts of kindness as good, because often much evil is committed by those whose intentions are good, is that not correct?"

"I suppose that is true," Amartanon answered.

"So when we say God is all good, and the Devil is all bad, do we not run into the same problem?"

Amartanon furrowed his brow and cocked his head. "No, we don't," he protested. "God is good. He is all good and he is everything good," he replied.

"I'm not saying he is, and I am not saying he is not," Solon answered. "I am simply saying you have never dared to consider the idea that he is not."

"But how could that be?" Amartanon asked.

"I want you to pay attention to what your body is feeling right now," Solon instructed. "You are feeling tense. Every fiber of your being is rejecting this idea completely. You do not even want to consider it. In fact, you want to dismiss me right now and you are in the grip of a terrible fear. *For this is the forbidden thought.* Very few people have the courage to consider it. They fear it as a terrible blasphemy and they fear God will become angry if they dare ask this question. Is that not what you are experiencing right now?"

Amartanon thought about this and he noticed that he did feel tension in his body and resistance in his mind. "I am," he said.

"Good. That admission is the first step. Now let me ask you, what kind of God would threaten you with harm for daring to think such a thing?"

"I don't know." Amartanon answered.

"Do you think a loving and kind God would strike you dead, or perhaps banish you to an eternity of suffering, simply because you considered this question? Think hard now. Is it not true that you fear exactly that?"

"I suppose I do," Amartanon said.

"Hmmm…" Solon said as he cocked his head to the side. "Interesting."

"So you are asking me to consider the idea that God is evil?"

"Yes, in a sense I am. I want to explore this idea and see where it might lead. Surely an all wise, omnipotent and loving God would not find this threatening in the least. There is no threat to him in this, any more than you are threatened by the thoughts of a tiny gnat."

"But we are not supposed to think such things," Amartanon protested.

"I know," Solon replied. "But isn't that odd? Why would God forbid us from thinking such a thing? Would he not be confident that such thoughts could only lead us to the conclusion that he is in fact all good? He would have nothing to fear in these questions, yet he is afraid. So much so that he threatens to destroy you if you dare entertain the thought. That sounds like a fearful and vengeful God. Not all loving. Not all good. That is conditional love. Agree with me or you shall suffer. There are *men* who have risen above such foolishness; certainly an all-good, all-loving God would have left such behaviors behind long ago. Why this approach?"

"We are to be obedient," Amartanon answered. "He wants us to choose to love him."

"I see," Solon replied. "Now why would an omnipotent God want that? Doesn't that sound like the tyrant who wants his subjects to love and worship him under threat of execution if they do not? This is a kind and loving God?"

Amartanon did not know how to answer this. Confusion consumed him. He felt naked and afraid. The deepest core of his being wanted to hide from these thoughts.

"Let us consider this deeply," Solon said. "Do not be afraid. You are free to reject these ideas completely should you choose to do so. But let's see where this thinking leads, shall we?"

Amartanon reluctantly nodded.

"We must now recap for a moment. We are speaking of God as if he is a person, but we have determined that God is really any act of kindness that manifests as a function of human action. But speaking of him as a person is helpful so long as we recognize that we are doing so. This means that the idea that 'God' can get angry with us is akin to saying that an act of kindness can get angry with us. But since we are attempting to explore these ideas, and since you have been taught to think of God as a person, this is necessary for the time being."

"Okay," Amartanon replied.

"So we can now say that the Devil is also something that comes into being each time a person commits an evil act, right?"

"That would be true," Amartanon answered.

"But just as with God, we have learned to think of the Devil as a person, so we will now speak of him in that manner."

"Okay."

"Let us consider then the idea that there really is a Devil. And let's assume this Devil really does want to corrupt the world. What would be the best way to manage that? What if he came up with the idea that, if he could convince the world that *he* was God and that *he* stood for everything true and good, and that *he* was all-loving and all-kind, this would be the best way to fool people into following him? People might cling to that idea, wanting the comfort of a God that was all-knowing and all-loving. Then he could issue proclamations such as, 'Thou shalt not kill.' This convinces the people that he is good and loving. But the very same God goes on to instruct his people, as in the book of Samuel, to '... go and smite Amalek, and utterly destroy all that they have, and spare them not; but slay both man and woman, infant and suckling, ox and sheep, camel and ass.' This is genocide committed by people following the instructions given by the very God who said 'Thou shalt not kill.' There is a severe contradiction here. But if we assume this God to be the Devil acting as an impostor who has tricked the people into believing him to be God, it makes perfect sense, does it not?"

Amartanon did not know how to answer this, so he said nothing.

"So now we have a God claiming to be all good, yet he instructs his people to commit genocide and kill innocent children who are still suckling at the breast of their mothers. Let us consider the possibility that such a God is in fact the Devil, because such an act is evil by any standard. The taking of innocent life is inherently bad, and if God instructed me to do so, I should have to deny him. This implies that I am morally superior to God, for I will not commit such an act even if He commands it of me. For this reason, I am going to assume this God to be no God at all. He is a Devil acting as God."

Amartanon turned to Mara. "This is crazy," he said.

"Is it?" Solon asked. "These things continue to this day. Take a look at war. Countries are forever going to war, setting out to kill, maim and rape in the name of 'God and Country.' You never hear such atrocities done in the name of 'Satan and Country.'"

Amartanon listened to these words not knowing what to say.

"And then this same God says, 'Thou shalt have no other Gods before me,' and he goes on to say, 'I am a jealous God.' Yet at the same time he would have us believe he is the only God. Why would the only God tell people to have no other God's before him? What would that God have to be jealous about? According to him, there are no other Gods, period. If he knew himself to be the only God, wouldn't he say something like, 'Don't invent fake Gods and worship them?' Or does he mean it is okay to have other gods so long as they do not come before him? Again, this makes no sense if he is the only God. And after Adam and Eve ate from the tree of the knowledge of good and evil, God says, 'Now the man has become like one of us and has knowledge of what is good and what is bad.' He is speaking of many Gods, not just himself as the only God. The story is fraught with contradiction. We can find more. For example, the eating of the fruit is thought to be a sinful act, a disobedient act and therefore Adam and Eve are to be punished. But prior to the eating of the fruit, they had no knowledge of good or evil, therefore they had no way of knowing that disobedience to God was evil. They are therefore punished for doing something evil when they had no idea what evil was or that evil even existed. We have already agreed that *intent* to do wrong was necessary if an act is to be considered evil. But here is poor Adam and Eve, with no knowledge of Good or Evil, who disobey God without intent, for they can have no intent to do evil if they do not know what evil is. The story sounds like a lie. This would be like telling a newborn baby not to cry, and then punishing it when it disobeys you. We do not do this because we are aware that the baby does not know right from wrong, therefore when it continues to cry in defiance of its mother's instruction, we cannot say it is being disobedient. We cannot say it is doing something for which it deserves punishment. We would think it a most evil and vile act to punish the baby for disobedience when it does not know what disobedience is. Yet this God inflicted punishment on Adam and Eve, two people who did not know right from wrong any more than a newborn infant knows right from wrong. They had no idea that disobeying God was a sin, yet they were punished as if they did know. Wouldn't this be just like the mother who spanks her newborn for disobeying her when she told it not to cry?"

"I suppose it would," Amartanon answered.

"Then once again we find that we are morally superior to this God, because we would not punish a person who had no idea that what they were doing was wrong."

"I hear what you are saying," Amartanon replied. "But... I..." He sighed heavily as he could not find words to express what he was feeling.

"Let us explore further," Solon said. "Next we find that there is the serpent, or the snake which first tempts Eve. God told them, 'Do not eat the fruit from this tree or you will die.' The snake tells them this is not true; you will not die. People have invented all kinds of stories to explain this because Adam and Eve ate of the fruit and they did not die. The snake was right. To rectify this glaring problem people make the claim that what God really meant was that Adam and Eve would have lived forever had they not listened to that evil snake, but now because they ate of the fruit of the tree they will 'someday' die. This is reading into the story—something one does to make sense of a story that is blatantly false. God said they would die. He did not say they would die some day off in the future. He did not say that they were immortal and eating the fruit would compromise that immortality. He said they would die. So let us consider the idea that God did in fact lie. That God did not want them to know good from evil, for if they came to know this, they might one day figure out he himself is evil. God goes on to curse the snake and make it the mortal enemy of man. But what was this snake really? Was it not the bringer of truth? Did it not expose the lie? And the snake has forever been known as the Ouroboros, the symbol of life, self-generating and eternal. That symbol is used in the medical profession to this very day with the snake wrapped around the staff. The staff represents the guiding hand of the shepherd, the snake the symbol of life. It represents the doctor guiding the forces of life. This serpent is evil? What if the reverse is true? Then all the discrepancies fall into place. The one we are told is God is a liar—he claims to be the only God though he knows this to be untrue. He then claims to be all-good, yet instructs people to commit all manner of evil in his name. Then Jesus came into the world, and if you find the texts the church thought they had destroyed, you find Jesus teaching this same thing. He claims to be the Son of God *and* the Son of Man. This implies that God is in man and that heaven resides in man too. It also makes sense when we consider our earlier idea that God is not an anthropomorphized being, but is instead a verb—an act of good that a human being does with the intent to do good. Then Jesus, as the son of man, is the embodiment of any good act done by man. Are you still with me here?"

"I think so," Amartanon answered.

"Jesus says these things in the Gospel of Thomas, one of the books the church thought destroyed. What if Jesus was telling people that the one you think of as God is not the real God; he is an impostor? Would not the church of his day want him crucified?

Killed in the name of their loving God? We still go to war in the name of this God and we have been told that this evil, prevaricating God and Jesus are one, so we go to war in the name of Jesus too, even though Jesus said, 'If your enemy smites your cheek, offer him the other.' It would seem that Jesus identified himself with the true God, the one that exists as that voice in the heart of every being, the one he most often referred to as the Father. This is the 'God' if you will that drives us to be good and kind; the God that comes into being when we act out of love and kindness. It is the other God that is in actuality the voice of the Devil; therefore we are not to listen to it. Jesus told people that the true Father exists inside of you; therefore you are morally superior to this impostor God. This is the forbidden thought. It is the thought of the heretic, the blasphemer. It is the thought you yourself never considered, even as you climbed the mountain and came to know the God, or the Father, that exists in you."

Amartanon's curiosity was now piqued. He felt resistance in his body, but these words seemed somehow compelling.

"Jesus goes on to call Peter 'The Rock.' And we are taught to believe this to mean that he is the rock upon which the Church of Jesus is built. But what if he meant that Peter was a rock in the sense that he was so hard-headed that Jesus' message could not penetrate into him? The banned Gospels speak of Jesus loving Mary Magdalene more than the others, and Peter becoming angry and jealous because Jesus loved a woman. This defied the teaching of the Devil impostor acting as God which said only men could be spiritual leaders. Therefore Peter would have none of it and he grew resentful. Even in the accepted Gospels, Jesus says to Peter, 'Get behind me, Satan! You are a stumbling block to me; you do not have in mind the things of God, but the things of men.' This is the very man who founded the church that we have all been taught to revere? The very man who then went on to deny Jesus three times before the cock crowed?

"Jesus never referred to any disciple as Satan except Peter. Perhaps Jesus knew that the church Peter would create in his name was going to be an impostor Church that would act in defiance of his teaching while doing so in his name.

"When you turn all of this around, it begins to make sense. But you have been taught these are the thoughts of the Devil. Turn it around and these so-called thoughts of the Devil become the voice of the true God inside of you, the one Jesus called the Father. This is the forbidden thought, the blasphemy—the very thing the church elders accused Jesus of doing."

Amartanon heard these words and was troubled. They bothered him. He did not want to consider them—not for the briefest moment. And yet something about them rang true.

Solon, recognizing this, spoke, "The Gospel of Thomas tells us that Jesus said, 'Let him who seeks continue seeking till he finds. When he finds he will become troubled. When he becomes troubled, he will be astonished and he will rule over all.' This is the true message of Jesus. Consider it, and see how things begin to change. Jesus goes on to say that not only is *he* the Son of God, *we are all*

Sons of God, the fruit of the same tree. We are the dismembered God who must be *re-collected*, as in recollect that which is already in us, and then we must *re-member* this dis-membered God as in 'Do this in *remembrance* of me.' And the one we have been taught to think of as the Devil? He was Lucifer, the beautiful angel of light; the bringer of light. Lucifer was cast down to the Earth. Did Jesus not say 'I am the light of the world'? Jesus also said, 'I and the Father are one.' What if the impostor God was the Devil and the one known as Lucifer was actually the true essence of God, the light *of* the world that exists *in* the world, in the hearts of all men? Could Jesus have been saying that Lucifer, the light giver, and I, the light giver, are one? It is entirely possible that you have had a lie embedded so deeply into your psyche that you fear even considering it for what it is."

Amartanon sat in silence, his soul wracked in agony. This *was* the forbidden thought. How could he possibly allow himself to consider it? Could the entire edifice upon which his understanding of the world have been corrupted by a Devil who convinced him that he, the Devil, was God?

Solon pointed at Mara and said, "Consider this Devil—*your* Devil—that you have been bound to since your entry into the valley, my son. What transgression did you commit in the name of your God so that you might enter here? What transgression bound you to this so-called Devil?"

Amartanon immediately remembered his violation of Sophia, but before he could speak, Solon continued.

"And from that moment on, this Devil has been with you. In the Gospel of Thomas, Jesus said, 'When the two become one, then you shall know me.' Perhaps it is time for you to follow your Devil, and to stop following your God."

"Are you saying that Mara and I are to become one?" Amartanon asked.

"I am not saying that," Solon answered. "And I am not, not saying that. I will leave that for you to work out. I am simply asking you to consider that which you have never considered; to question that which you have never questioned; to look at that which you have never allowed yourself to see. In this way, perhaps, you will come to know the true nature of your being."

Amartanon's head spun. It was as if the rug had been yanked forcefully from beneath his feet. He felt himself drifting with nothing to cling to. It was maddening.

"Let me tell you another story. This one is much older than your stories of Jesus. It is an ancient Hindu story," Solon continued, his voice softening. "It is the story of the Hindu God Prajmapati."

"Ok." Amartanon replied weakly, his mind still reeling from the information just given him.

"In the Hindu story, Prajmapati was considered the first of all Gods—the only God, if you will. He is spoken of in the ancient Vedic texts. He was known as the ultimate creator God, the 'Lord of all creation who became man.' He is said to have given his life's blood to pay the penalty for our sins and to impart to us eternal life. He was the original creator and he was alone. He wanted companions so he created lesser Gods to commune with. These Gods began to resent his powers and wanted to be the rulers of all, so, they ganged up on Prajmapati and tore him into almost infinite little pieces. It was this act that gave rise to the Universe. To the Hindu people, the Universe is comprised of the dismembered and scattered pieces of the original creator God. Today we might consider this God to be the atoms from which all of creation is comprised.

"The lesser Gods then set themselves up as the Gods of the world, each posturing for supremacy." Solon paused for a moment. "Now let us compare this story to the account of God as told in the Bible. The Biblical God said—and we must ask to whom he said it— 'Now this man has become like *us* knowing good from evil.' According to the Hindu story, this makes sense. The God of the Old Testament would be similar to one of these lesser Hindu Gods who dismembered Prajmapati, tore him apart and spread him about so as to create the universe as we know it. He set himself up above all the other Gods, speaking of those less powerful than he. It also makes sense that he would then proclaim that, "Thou shalt have no other Gods before me," as he knew the other Gods to exist, but claimed himself to be the strongest amongst them. He would also know that human beings, being made as they are of the dismembered parts of the original creator God Prajmapati, are themselves expressions of Prajmapati, therefore they are superior to he. He would also know that human beings are a threat to him as a lesser God because should they ever remember that they are the essence of the creator God himself, he would no longer have any power over them. Understand that I am now speaking of the Biblical God in his self-proclaimed role of creator of all. I am telling you this to show you how the earlier Hindu story was taken and corrupted into the Biblical story of God. We can see this when we look at the similarities in the two stories.

"Let us now return to the Hindu story. The people of the day knew these Gods to be impostors, but they also knew them to be powerful and easily angered. Because of this, they made offerings to the Gods, most often in the form of ghee which is clarified butter. They did not do this as an act of worship. It was an appeasement, much like a tribute paid to a king, so that he would not cause the person making the offering any harm. This was, in their minds, a necessary business transaction that was made to bring about certain desired effects from the Gods, such as a plentiful harvest or good health, for example. The people did not like these Gods and they felt themselves to be oppressed by them. They believed they had a duty to the primary creator God himself—Prajmapati." Solon leaned forward in his chair, his eyes gleaming with excitement. "Now here is where the story gets interesting," he said.

"The duty the people had to Prajmapati was to 'recollect' and to 'remember.' We think of recollection and remembering as a mental process as in, 'I recollect the time when...' or 'I remember that.' These people thought of recollecting and remembering as mental processes as well, but they added to them a physical aspect—an aspect we have forgotten today, much as they believed themselves to have forgotten back then. What was forgotten was simply this: that Prajmapati was in everything and everyone. The true God existed in all people, therefore it was the task of the people to recollect this fact, but more than that, the mental act of recollecting was also the means through which the scattered pieces of Prajmapati were re-collected, or brought together. From there the people were to remember him, and in so doing the physical act of re-membering the dismembered body of Prajmapati was accomplished. And it was accomplished in the soul of the human-being who was able to remember and therefore re-member this God in himself.

"Thus the one who re-collected and then re-membered realized the ultimate fact, that he and Prajmapati were one. This is much like Jesus saying 'I and the Father are one.' And it is exactly the same as Jesus who said, 'Do this in remembrance of me.' You see, even Jesus said to re-member the essence of him, the Christ essence, the Prajmapati essence, the original creator God essence in you. Once this is accomplished, the lesser Gods lose all power and death is overcome. But let me be very clear here. Death is not overcome by this body or this person I think of as 'me' living forever. It is not that at all. This realization results in the one who is aware, recognizing that this manifestation he thinks of as himself is nothing but a temporary manifestation of Prajmapati. It will dissolve into the particles from which it formed and the entity I think of as me will disappear with it—utterly. There is no life hereafter in which I continue to exist as me in some spirit form. There is a transference of the very essence or idea of 'me' so that the self *is* Prajmapati, and it is that self that lives forever. This is the true eternal life. The idea of the self is dissolved and transfigured into the identity of the eternal God, the creator God, the true God."

Solon leaned back in his chair and smiled. "But I must caution you," he continued. "This is the so-called 'secret knowledge.' It has existed in every religious teaching throughout the history of human kind, but it has been reserved only for those who are ready to hear it. There is great danger in this teaching for those caught in the grip of their egos. People who are not ready for this begin to think, 'I am God,' when the true message is not that at all. The true realization is that 'God is,' and he is now expressing through me as he has expressed, and continues to express, through all things whether we know it or not.

"So when Jesus said, 'Do this in remembrance of me,' it was an instruction to do the very thing the people who 're-membered' Prajmapati did. The rite of communion is the eating of his body and the drinking of his blood just as the parts of Prajmapati were 're-collected' and then 're-membered' in the bodies of the people of that day. And through this act we *become* him, or more accurately, we become the essence that also once manifested as him. It matters not which religion a person chooses. Think of religions as languages, each a different tongue through which the same story is told—but only to those who are ready to hear."

Solon turned to Mara and said, "This man saw a vision of the ancient script, the most holy of the holy texts, did he not?"

"He did," Mara answered nodding.

"I must interrupt," Amartanon said. "I do not see what that ancient text has to do with any of this. And I am not sure what you want me to think. Am I to believe Prajmapati actually exists?"

Solon's eyes narrowed, his face grew stern, then it relaxed into a pleasant smile. "That text," he said, "tells the entire story. It matters not what you believe. It matters only that you begin to experience it. Think of the Prajmapati story as metaphor, if you like. Think of it as actually happening, if you find that helps. Think of the new telling of the Bible stories that I just spoke as absolutely true, or as metaphor. These are nothing but tools in that even they are to be abandoned in favor of what actually is."

"I still don't understand," Amartanon protested.

"In the text that you read in your vision, you read of the 'Always Is' imagining itself as the many things. Is this not like Prajmapati being scattered about so that the universe came to be? He then lost himself in the many things. Is this not like the forgetting man has done? Then he experienced the power of the word, and with this power came all manner of distractions in which the Always Is lost itself even further. Is this not like the lesser Gods that now rule the universe, or the imposter God of the Bible? Is this not like our earlier discussion where we attempted to find absolute definitions of Good and Evil, only to find that the words themselves were inadequate and could not actually accomplish an absolute understanding of the very concepts they represent? It is the word that controls the thought; and it is this that must be overcome if thought is to free itself into the reality of that which is."

Solon gestured toward Mara as he spoke to Amartanon. "You come into this valley with your Devil in tow. I tell you when the two become one, then you will know me. You then assume that I mean you and Mara. That assumption, though ultimately correct, is like putting the cart before the horse. Perhaps I should have said that first the three must become two, then the two will become one. But here we are again limited by the true devils—words. Have you not heard how deceitful the Devil is? That the Devil mixes truth with untruth to keep you fooled? Nothing does this better than words. Every word I have spoken is true, but they are also not true. Or at least not the full truth. They are a mixture of truth and untruth—how can they be anything but? They are not the things themselves; words are only the symbols we have applied to things, so a word may *represent* a thing, but it can never *be* the thing. You sit here in my home and you have listened to nothing but sound waves shaped in various ways so as to convey an idea. Neither the words nor the ideas they represent are real. They are both abstractions. If you seek an idea you will be forever grasping at thin air. You can never catch the air in your hand, and you can never capture an idea with your mind. It will slip through the fingers of your mind and you will be left searching yet again. This is what you have done and this is the source of your frustration."

"I am not inclined to believe any of this," Amartanon replied.

"Ah," Solon exclaimed. "You now want to contradict *my* words with *your* words. Let me save you some time. None of my words are true. There. You win." Solon smiled.

An exasperated look came over Amartanon. "What...?"

"Do not look for truth in words, my friend. Look beyond them."

"So by moving beyond words I will find the truth?" Amartanon asked.

"You might say that," Solon said. But in saying that, you will find that there is no truth. But by saying that you will find that to say 'there is no truth' is itself a statement of truth, thus it contradicts itself. And there you will find the dead end that all words lead to in the end. Thus you will be confronted with the choice—your choice—that will bring into being whatever you choose."

Amartanon strained to make sense of this but he could not.

Solon turned to Mara. "He let you bring him here. Perhaps now he will follow you." He turned to Amartanon. "Follow this devil of yours my friend; you never know what you might find."

Mara spoke, "I was thinking of taking him to visit the caves. May we trouble you for a couple of torches?"

"I think that a splendid idea," Solon replied smiling. "Let me get them for you and the two of you may be on your way." Solon exited the room then returned shortly. "Here you are my friends. And stop looking so troubled," he said taking Amartanon by the shoulders and gently shaking him. "All is as it should be. No need for worry." Solon hugged him and the two departed.

CHAPTER 8

The two walked in silence for some time, Mara now leading the way. Amartanon's soul was disturbed and deeply troubled. Solon's words echoed in his mind, though he could make no sense of them. The sun had set behind the horizon, and darkness descended upon the valley. Amartanon thought of how the well-lit places that he once saw so clearly were now lost to him in the darkness. And he began to experience a disconcerting sensation. It was something deep in his gut demanding to be heard. People tend to think with the mind, sometimes with the heart. But the stomach must be heard too, for it is here that the instinct toward survival finds its source. He wondered, "Am I a brain that evolved a stomach so that I might continue to survive? Or am I a stomach that evolved a brain so that I might be better able to find food?" He knew not the answer to this question, but he did know that his gut was speaking to him now. Amartanon did not want to hear it, and he fought hearing it though he was not fully aware of doing so. He experienced this discord as a mild agitation, ephemeral, something that hovered in his mind finding no firm ground upon which to land. It was the voice of that thing, so deep inside him that he no longer believed it existed; therefore to listen to it would require that he admit it was there, but this he was not ready to do. He was, after all, the man who had climbed the highest mountain. He had scaled the heights and was able to rise above all, to see the things no other had seen. Why did he feel something was still missing? What could possibly be missing? He became aware that these questions were permeating his mind. He railed against these thoughts, for they did not sit well with who he thought himself to be. He wanted to shove them back into that forgetful place where he kept all of those things too painful to allow into the full light of awareness. This was the source of his discomfort. That which he refused to see demanded to be seen. The war now raged inside of him, yet he managed to avoid thinking of it. He did this by reminding himself of all that he knew. His faith in his knowledge comforted him.

Soon the words of Solon began taking a new shape in Amartanon's mind. He now told himself that Solon was a silly old man who lived in a hut. His words were nothing but the words of a fool. "I was a fool for having listened to them," he thought. He began to feel better as he reconstructed the events in such a way as to fit with what he already wanted to believe. "Why should I be troubled by the words of a fool?" he thought, but as he thought it, he also spoke it without realizing he had done so.

"That is a good question," Mara replied.

"What?" Amartanon said confused. "Oh, I suppose I was thinking out loud."

"The challenge," Mara continued, "Is in identifying the fool."

"Solon is the fool," Amartanon snapped. His tone surprised even him.

"I see," Mara answered, not caring that Amartanon's tone grew harsh. "But, may I ask," Mara continued, "What if you are mistaken? What if *you* are the fool?"

Anger verging on rage swelled in Amartanon. "Are you calling me a fool?" he snapped.

"No," Mara replied. "I am asking you to consider something. You believe that you know the truth, therefore Solon's words are those of a fool. I am simply asking, what if Solon's words are true, and it is you that is being the fool. How would you know? How does one ever know?"

"I know the truth," Amartanon replied, "and God is not the Devil."

"I hear you," Mara responded. "But if I were to speak to Solon, he might say the same thing; that he knows the truth and God *is* the Devil. How would I determine which one of you is correct, and which of you is mistaken?"

Amartanon thought about this question. It was a most difficult question to answer, but an answer came. "He believes what he believes, and I believe what I believe," he said.

Mara smiled. "Do you take the time to listen to the words you speak?" he asked.

"What do you mean?"

"Just a moment ago, you said you know the truth. Now you are saying it is nothing more than your *belief*. What is it that you possess? Is it *knowledge* of something? Or is it simply a *belief in* something? If it is a belief, then is it not simply your assertion of that which you want to be true whether it is true or not?"

"No," Amartanon protested. "What I have is knowledge."

"But Solon would say that what he has is knowledge. So again I must ask, which of you should I believe?"

"I don't care who you believe," Amartanon snapped. "You are free to believe whomever you wish."

"That is a cowardly answer," Mara stated flatly. "You are avoiding my question with that response."

"So now you are calling me a coward?" Amartanon asked, his anger seething.

Mara stopped dead in his tracks. He turned to face Amartanon and stared directly into his eyes, his own eyes narrowing with resolve. "Yes," he stated firmly, un-waveringly. "I am saying this directly to your face, that you, my friend, are a coward."

Amartanon stared back at Mara, his rage fuming, their eyes locked in a silent battle. But Mara would not relent, and Amartanon felt his position weakening in the energy of Mara's steely resolve. Mara, sensing this, spoke.

"You are caught in the *belief* that you know the truth," he said. His voice was firm, but compassionate. Amartanon sensed Mara was not angry and this caused his own anger to relent. "Because of this rock-solid belief you have, you will not allow into your mind any information that does not agree with what you already believe. It is for this reason, and this reason alone, that *you* are the fool. And let me tell you something," Mara continued, "It is not a bad thing to be a fool. We are all fools from time to time. But it can be quite damaging to be the fool without realizing it. You speak from the position of 'knowing the truth' and you act as if you know it absolutely. Solon speaks only from his 'experience of the truth' and therefore does not believe that he knows anything. He has an experience to share, not knowledge to impart. This is the fundamental difference between you and he. Solon is open to anything because he recognizes experience to be entirely personal; therefore there is nothing to be stated absolutely. You are open to nothing because you already think you know, therefore you will only allow in that which reinforces your preconceived beliefs."

Amartanon stared into Mara's eyes. He wanted to find anger there. He wanted to find contempt. But he could not. Mara's eyes spoke the truth of Mara, and they exuded nothing but pure compassion. He realized that he had never before looked deeply into Mara. He now saw in him that which he never realized was there. He thought Mara to be nothing more than an irritation, an inconvenience bound to him throughout this journey. He had not trusted Mara, and he thought Mara might be out to hurt him as devils are prone to do.

But now he stood mesmerized by Mara's eyes, and he saw in them—no, he did not see—he felt something. What was it? He focused his attention on his body as opposed to the thoughts in his mind, and he found there a deep compassion—Mara's compassion…Mara's compassion was somehow infecting him, giving itself over to him. It was an absolute expression, beautiful and pristine, something deeper than anything he had ever before experienced because it was in the body and Amartanon had hitherto experienced things only in his mind. He realized he had never before had an actual experience—at least not one like this, not one that was wholly in his body. His experiences before had been those of the words he used to describe experiences, as if words stood between him and anything visceral, real. It made him uncomfortable such that he wanted to reflexively pull away, yet he longed for it just the same. It was a feeling that seemed somehow soothing.

Amartanon allowed himself to soften just a bit, still staring into Mara's eyes. As he did so, he began to feel something moving deep within himself. There was, at the core of his being, an emotion rising. It was something warm and comforting, yet at the same time he felt a sense of fear too. An awareness grew that spoke to him, comforted him, telling him that, though he feared this new feeling, whatever it was, all was well. He realized that he feared this sensation so deeply that he had never allowed himself to truly feel it before, even though, he now knew, the experience had tried to make itself felt numerous times before. What was this emotion that felt so peaceful and comforting, yet frightening at the same time?

SOPHOS

A word began to take shape in the darkest recesses of his mind. "Love," it said. He did not resist it this time. He allowed it into his awareness. "I am feeling love," he thought. But this time it was not the abstract love that existed only in his head—that tired and dead thing he had felt so many times before. This was deeper, warmer, and it exuded from his body independently of all thought. This was the true love of pure being manifesting itself in every cell, every sinew. It was a fleshy love that glowed like a warm fire whose flame did not burn, but instead comforted.

Mara, sensing this, smiled. "Now you are beginning to see," he said. "You need not say anything, for words will add nothing but they will take much. Simply let yourself be in the experience; fully in the experience…for you are that which you feel."

Amartanon smiled. His eyes glowed with wonder.

"We are nearing the caves," Mara said. "But it is dark and we need rest. Let us take the time to sleep here in the darkness. One need not always seek the light. You will now find the darkness to be quite comforting. You will begin to recognize the power, and even the necessity, of that which is not."

These words confused Amartanon, but he knew better than to worry about them. Where confusion had always before been a problem to be resolved, it seemed now to be an opportunity to embrace. It dawned on him that confusion will resolve itself if one will but let it.

The two found a spot of soft grass to lie on, and they bedded down for the night. The cat curled up next to Amartanon to sleep.

He stroked the cat lovingly. He stared up at the stars twinkling in the darkened sky. He thought of the vastness of the universe, and as he did, a feeling of insignificance in the small dot of matter that he thought of as himself in the face of this wealth of distance and size overwhelmed him. This was a feeling that, though he only now became fully aware of it, had always existed within him.

The thought came to him, "Where does one search for the light?" The answer then followed, "Why, in the dark, of course. One never looks for light in the light for it is already there." He then recognized the impossibility of this, as light cannot be found in darkness for if the light was there, it would not be dark. He then began to realize that one does not search for the light; one instead carries the light into the darkness. He began to see himself as the light. Then he knew that light is awareness, and wherever awareness was, light was too. He pondered this. He wondered where the thought came from. As he thought about it, he became increasingly aware that he was not the originator of the thought. He had never been the originator of any thought. Thoughts instead simply came to him, and he assigned himself ownership of them after the fact as if he had been the one thinking them. Questions, then the answers to the questions, simply appeared in his mind—planted there by an awareness that transcended that which he thought himself to be.

These were unusual thoughts and feelings, and they produced inside of him a tendency toward apprehension. It was as if the act of considering these ideas evidenced an insanity that had infected his mind. He heard a cricket chirping in the cool, night air. The sound spoke to him as it had never spoken before. He felt each waft of the cool night air caressing him, and he felt it fully as he had never felt anything before. He was alive—fully alive with a cacophony of sensations swirling about. He became aware that, even though he was not the originator of thoughts, the originator of thoughts was something that had always been with him, surrounding him, within him, without him, a part of him though somehow separate from him. He realized that the originator of thoughts had a voice and that he had been taught not to listen to that voice; that the world demanded instead that he conform to the illusions of those around him in defiance of the voice. He then knew that, even though he had thought himself to have risen above all of this nonsense, he was still acting out of that nonsense—albeit in a more subtle way than before. His mind thus opened. His body softened. He was no longer a rock; he had instead become a far more fluid thing. Even that was not entirely accurate. He never was a rock. He had always been fluid, but through the use of words, that incessant dialog forever infecting his mind, he had convinced himself that he was a solid thing even though he was not. With this shift in his perception, his reality changed.

It was here, with these thoughts, that he hit the inevitable dead-end one always comes to with words. All words, if you ponder them long enough and deeply enough will lead you to contradictions. This is their great power, and their great deception—both at the same time. For the truth one seeks exists within the contradiction itself. It is there that one must abandon words and relax into the experience of that which cannot be understood. To hang onto the word at that point requires that a person make a choice that reality is this or it is that, effectively abandoning the contradiction entirely. That is where dogma begins, and that is where words tempt us to impose *on* reality that which is not *in* reality.

He began to see the proper use of words. He thought to himself, "I must use them to bring me to the contradiction—then abandon them once I arrive." For it is at this point, he now saw, that experience, and experience only, is the teacher, the guide. "We abhor contradiction," he thought. "Our entire science is predicated on the belief or - dare I even think it - the *faith* that contradictions cannot exist?" This was the deep conditioning that he carried, as do nearly all people. He had been taught that contradictions are a consequence of improper logic, or misguided thinking. Because of this, he attempted to resolve all contradictions believing that they represented some mistake that therefore obscured his view of reality. It never occurred to him that reality *was* the contradiction. The contradiction presented him with a choice in which he felt compelled to choose one or the other of the contradictory propositions because he believed they could not both be true. In so doing, his choice collapsed the 'what might be' into the 'what now is,' creating the illusion that he believed to be reality. It was an experience of a reality based upon a flawed choice, because either choice had to be flawed, as it was always only half of the reality. Making the opposite choice would not have been any better, because it too was flawed. No, the answer lies in accepting both contradictory positions at once. In this he found his true power. For knowing this, he was now able to make the choice with awareness, recognizing that the choice made did not represent a reality discovered. It was instead a preference chosen. It represented a reality that he actively brought into being. It was the act of choosing one over the other according to his preference, nothing more. But the other reality existed also; therefore he knew both even as he chose one. This was his creative power in which the words could be refashioned in any image he chose, and could be reconstructed any time he wanted.

The thought then came to him that he knew nothing. How could he know anything when there was nothing to know? How could he know anything when reality was nothing more than a personal choice between two contradictory positions? All so-called knowledge was nothing more than an arrangement of words that resulted in certain predictable patterns when they are first held to the rules established by the imposition of some arbitrary set of assumptions. Those assumptions being the choice one made of believing either this or that when the contradiction was reached. By choosing this, an entirely logical philosophy would follow. By choosing that, another entirely logical philosophy would follow. But neither could be true, because both rested on the faith in choosing this *over* that, or that *over* this, when *both* this and that are true, or *neither* this nor that are true. Each choice is nothing but an arbitrary decision. There is never an absolute truth to be discovered, only a choice to be made as to what will become true. With this newfound awareness, he cured himself of the disease of knowledge—the disease that manifests as the choice that denies the act of choosing by disguising itself as a "thing" that was discovered as if it somehow existed independently of the choice made. He was, at long last, able to learn, because he now realized that reality was an interaction—something that came to be as opposed to something that exists independently of him.

The following morning they awoke to the sound of birds singing in the trees. It was the beautiful melody of life expressing as life tends to do. A cool breeze blew gently caressing their faces. Amartanon sat up, still groggy and still lost in his thoughts from the night before. He took a moment to feed the cat that slept beside him through the night. He looked to Mara, who now appeared more a friend and less an adversary.

"It all leads to contradiction," he said.

Mara's eyes darted up suddenly, surprised. "This is true," he said smiling. "All descriptions of reality lead to contradiction."

"I see that now," Amartanon replied. "There is, at the core of everything, a choice."

"That is the thing people do not like," Mara answered. "At the core of every belief system is a choice. There is no right or wrong choice; it is simply a matter of preference as to which choice we make. That, in turn, leads to a feeling of uncertainty. It is this uncertainty that causes deep anxiety. People then seek to calm this anxiety by finding others who agree with them, as if in agreement they will find comfort. But this comfort is doomed to fail as it is not in accord with reality. Reality is the simple fact that the choice is a purely personal endeavor. You do it simply because you want to, then you seek affirmation from others that it was the right thing to do. When you see this process for what it is, you become freed from group-think, and you embrace the freedom to choose as you please, and to change your mind tomorrow should you choose to do so. But this leads to a feeling of uncertainty and vulnerability. It is that unprotected place of complete freedom. People seem to like the *idea* of freedom, not the *reality* of it. The reality of it carries with it a greater burden of responsibility than most people are comfortable assuming. Thus, out of fear, they seek agreement so as to convince themselves that the choice they made was no choice at all—it was a discovery. This need drives them, and to satisfy it, they act as if the choice was made for them, thus they give themselves over to slavery. This is how dogma is born. Dogma is always a form of slavery as it demands of you that you never choose, you instead agree with whatever it is some authority has chosen for you. You thus give away the only power you ever had—the power to choose for yourself. I take it you are beginning to see this now?"

"I am," Amartanon replied.

Mara smiled. "I am," he said, "the spoken word of God."

Amartanon stared at Mara, his mind absorbing every word.

"If you look deeply enough into the core of your being," Mara said. "You will find there the deepest of all contradictions. You are yourself, at your very core, a contradiction. You are the essence of God experiencing this life as a man. There is no deeper contradiction than the realization that you are, in fact, both. And with that realization comes the ultimate choice. Which would you prefer to express in this reality? You can be either one you choose any time you choose to be so."

Amartanon nodded his understanding.

"Imagine, if you will, the time before all of this existed. Imagine the black nothingness of the absolute void. Nothing was. Then, out of this absolute nothingness, God had the thought, 'I am.' Then BOOM! The big bang happened and it suddenly came to be. It was the first thought, and with it came the awareness of self. With that came the material world. *You* are the originator of that thought; and…you are a man experiencing yourself within it. You are both. This is the first understanding. From here it all becomes your playground to experience as you like. But that is what it always was. Nothing has changed. This is the way."

"But I must ask," Amartanon replied, "what about ethics? If we are all absolutely free to do anything we want, would not anarchy ensue?"

Mara smiled. "Look deeply into yourself and see if you can find the answer to that question within you. You are beginning to see that you, and the thing you have always thought of as God, are the same. You are nothing but one particular expression of that God essence. But as you begin to see this, you also see that all other people are manifestations of the very same essence that is manifesting as you. What happens to your concept of moral or ethical behavior when you begin to see this?"

Amartanon pondered this question. "I cannot harm another, because there is no other than me to harm," he answered.

"Exactly," Mara replied. "For that reason, ethical behavior moves from *compulsory* to *compelling*. You no longer engage in ethical behavior because it is expected of you. You instead express it because it makes no sense to do otherwise. That is true freedom."

Amartanon had nothing more to say. He let the words of Mara melt into him. He did not attempt to understand them. He simply absorbed into his being the essence that traveled with the words. It was the essence of Mara flowing through the word into the reality of him. He felt the mingling of those essences, his and Mara's. He knew himself to be something other than that which he had ever known before. The fear of uncertainty subsided. The peace of the acceptance of what is became him. The caterpillar was turning into a butterfly, and he knew it.

CHAPTER 9

"There is someone you must now see," Mara said solemnly. "There is a cave just ahead. I will give you a torch and you will enter alone. I cannot follow you there. This is something you must do on your own."

Mara stood so as to suggest it was time to move on. Amartanon stood and followed Mara to the cave, the cat following behind.

"Here is your torch," Mara said as he lit it and handed it to Amartanon. "There is the entrance to the cave. Someone is waiting for you in there."

Amartanon turned to face the cave. He drew a deep breath to calm the anxiety trying to take hold of him and he entered. He did not hesitate. Any fear that tried to arise in him was left in his mind so that his body would not react. He was moving into his destiny.

SOPHOS

He walked in the darkness lit only by the flickering flame of his torch. Soon he heard a woman weeping ahead. He eased toward the sound, and the narrow path opened into a large cavern. At the center of the cavern he saw a woman weeping as she lay prone on the floor, chains binding her in her prison. He approached and laid his hand on her shoulder.

"Are you okay?" he asked.

The woman lifted her head and turned to him. He recognized her immediately as Sophia. He was surprised, then not surprised. "Why are you crying?" he asked.

Sophia looked up at him through the tears in her eyes. "Because I am imprisoned here. This is *your* doing. Why are you doing this to me?"

Amartanon stared at her. He knew instantly the truth of her words. He did not resist them; he instead settled himself into them. He observed the words as they began to grow in him, mingle with him, become him. He felt deep compassion welling from within. There was also a fleeting sensation of shame and guilt. His mind considered locking onto those, then thought better of it.

"I have come here to free you," he said. "I am here to set right that which I have wronged. I do not yet know how to do this, but I feel myself very close to learning. I see now the consequence of my action and I will rectify this."

Sophia stared into his eyes. She began to shine with a radiant brilliance.

"You have come to free me when it is I who will free you," she said.

Amartanon stared at her puzzled, unable to grasp the meaning of her words. "What do you mean?" he asked.

135

"People seek freedom through knowledge," she replied. "Knowledge is a useful tool, but it will only carry you so far."

"I don't understand…"

"Wisdom is the awareness of that which you do not know," Sophia continued. "It is an opening up of the realm of possibilities. In your knowledge, you think you know, therefore you harden into a stone. In wisdom you will begin to see that you do not know, therefore you become soft and pliable, open to that which is new to you, that which, as a stone, exists but you cannot see. Those who know everything can learn nothing."

Amartanon felt a familiar stirring deep in his soul, but he was aware of it this time and he did not resist it.

"I have much to learn, don't I?"

Sophia smiled, tears of agony streaming down her cheeks. "Yes," she said, "but the most important thing you must still learn is how to unlearn. When you master that, I will be freed from this prison in which you have bound me. On that day, I shall stand beside you and we will be as one."

Amartanon stared blankly, his mind lost in thought.

"What is it?" Sophia asked.

A pained look came over his face. "I see you bound by these chains to that steel ring drilled into the rocky floor, and I hear you telling me that I did this to you, but I have no recollection of doing so. How is this my doing?"

"You think you know. You worship knowledge. This is why I named you Amartanon. It is a Greek name that means 'fool.'

Knowledge comes from intellect, and intellect is a thing of the head. Wisdom comes from the heart, and it is wisdom that you lack. When you entered the valley, you violated your wisdom in the pursuit of knowledge preferring as you do the one over the other. That act bound me here in this darkness. This is your great mistake. You want to think your way out, but you cannot think your way out of this. You must *feel* your way. You must let go of all knowledge and embrace not-knowing. Only then will you begin to hear the inner voice that speaks softly in the recesses of the heart. It is the heart that will guide you where the head cannot go."

"But if I do this of which you speak, I will certainly be a fool," he protested.

"You are mistaken," Sophia corrected him. "You still think of a fool as someone who is stupid or uneducated, but this is not so. A fool is but a person who lacks wisdom. Many fools are very intelligent and very well educated. But they often do the most foolish things. It is wisdom that you lack, and this is the source of the name I bestowed upon you—the source of that which you have chosen to be."

Amartanon stared into her eyes. They exuded a desperate pleading that he longed to set right. And he saw in them something more—something other. He wondered what it was. He then saw the answer. She loved him, him…exactly as he was and in a way that he was incapable of doing therefore he was unable to love her as she loved him. He wanted to love her but something barred him from doing so.

"I am the cause of your suffering?" he asked.

"Yes," she replied, her voice choking as the pain of her love tore at her heart.

Amartanon felt her pain. It descended upon him like a heavy fog, thick and hard to breathe. It was more than he could bear, for it carried with it the weight of his responsibility. He felt her pain, and he wanted to ease it, but that which was needed to ease it was not yet in him. He felt that too.

"What..." he strained to speak, but her tears had become his own. He looked away, the burden that had fallen upon him was nearly too great to bear. He looked back to Sophia. He wanted to resolve this, to fix it, to do something, anything. "What am I to do?" he asked weakly.

"I cannot answer that," Sophia replied. "You must find the answers within you."

He felt the overwhelming sensation of worthlessness.

"I know not the nature of my own soul," he said.

"You will," Sophia reassured him.

"And if I don't?" he asked.

"Then I shall die," she said and she turned her head to cry.

He gently stroked her hair. This was an unbearable burden to him. He knew, down to the deepest depths of his being, that his mistakes caused Sophia to suffer. He despised himself. He knew himself to be something other than he thought himself to be and he hated it—*hated it!* "What kind of man does this?" he thought. "What am I?" Then he stopped himself because he knew that even this would cause her further pain. Self-flagellation would not help

Sophia. He had to make this right, and the only way to do that was to make himself right.

"I must leave you here," he said. As he spoke, a surge of hopelessness overwhelmed him for he did not know if it was in him to do that which must be done. He threw himself on the ground beside her sobbing.

Sophia lifted her chained arms and struggled to embrace him, to comfort him. "You can do this," she said softly, lovingly. "You must do it. It is your destiny."

He looked up at her. "I don't know where to begin," he pleaded.

"That which is not in you must be sought elsewhere," she said. "If you connect to the source, you will find in that source the strength you need."

"I…I can't…"

"Yes you can," Sophia reassured him.

Amartanon gathered himself together and stood. "I don't know what must be done, nor do I know how to do it. But if there is a way I shall find it," he said. Sophia stared into his eyes saying nothing. He could not look upon her any longer, his shame was too great.

"I will fix this somehow," he said. Panic filled him and his shame tempted him to run, to hide, to forget her and deny she even existed. But that feeling passed. He looked down upon her again swallowing his pride, his shame, his guilt.

"I must leave you now," he said, "But know that I will come for you soon." He reached down and touched her hair, then he turned from her and left her in the cave. Sophia wept softly in the darkness.

"You saw her?" Mara asked as Amartanon emerged, the bright light of the sun searing his eyes.

"I did," he replied.

"And?"

"I must make this right," he said. "I do not know how to do this, but I must find a way. I only hope the answers will come."

"It is a funny thing," Mara said, "It was in the pursuit of knowledge that you imprisoned her. It is as if hiding something in the darkness makes it so it never existed. You saw her as an impediment to your progress, so, you violated her. Then you cut her from your being. From that moment onward you lived a half-truth expressed through your half a life."

Amartanon stared at Mara. A thought of anger formed in his mind, but he saw it forming and did not let it move into his body. The thought found no fertile soil so it simply dissipated into the nothingness from whence it came. He thought this odd. He saw that thoughts need the energy in his body if they are to overwhelm him, and that he did not have to give this energy over to them. He also saw that words formed in his mind, but they were not his words—or rather, he was beginning to see that words were a product of thought and that no thought was ever his. Thoughts just popped into his head outside of his control. He realized that, just as sights come to the eye and sounds come to the ear, thoughts come to the mind. We do not create them. We are not the originator of them. They come, and then we claim them as our own.

"I am beginning to see," Amartanon began, "that thoughts are sensory impressions like any other sensory impressions."

"What do you mean?" Mara asked.

"I feel myself beginning to observe," he answered. "As the observer, I pay attention to the impressions coming to me. I am beginning to realize that I have never done this before."

Mara stared at him curiously.

"It is as if I never really saw anything," Amartanon continued. "I never heard anything. I never felt, tasted or smelled anything." He strained to find words to describe this experience. "That's not exactly right," he said. "I would see something, but then I immediately started a dialog in my mind so that I was describing it to myself as opposed to fully experiencing it. I am beginning to simply experience that which I see, hear, touch... But there is no longer the 'me' thinking, seeing, hearing, touching, smelling. These are simply happening, then I assume that somehow I am doing it, that I am causing it but I am not causing it at all. There is not even an "I" there to do anything. It is simply happening and I am flowing out of it, not causing it. It is the same as before, only different."

"I see," Mara replied. "Do you need words?"

"Do I need them?" Amartanon asked while pondering the question. "I suppose not," he said. "They are useful when trying to convey an experience to another, but they are not needed as far as the experience within me goes. Thoughts now seem different to me. They seem more like any other sensory experience. I am learning to observe them without reacting to them."

"Ah…" Mara replied. "You are beginning to see that the thought is not you."

"Yes," Amartanon said, pleased that Mara understood. "It seems to me that thoughts are simply another form of information coming in from the environment. They no longer seem to be mine; therefore I can listen to them. They feel more like instructions…or perhaps temptations. No, that's not quite right."

"I understand," Mara said. "Words cannot adequately describe this realization. They are unable to fully describe any experience. They are merely approximations. But I can say this…by separating your sense of self from your thoughts, you cease being a slave to them and you become instead the master over them."

"Yes, that's it," Amartanon said.

"Are you feeling okay?" Mara asked.

"What do you mean?"

"Your experience with Sophia just now, that had to be difficult."

Amartanon's eyes turned downward. "Yes," he said. It was difficult. I've done a terrible thing, Mara," he said. "I must make this right."

"Do you think you can make it right?"

"I don't know," he answered. "I hope so."

"I have something to show you," Mara said, changing the subject. "I think you are ready to see it now. There is another cave just ahead. Let us go there." Mara turned and led the way. He followed a path that led into a heavily forested area, the white cat trailing happily behind. Rays of sunlight pierced the canopy of leaves such that tiny specks of light dotted the ground. The air grew still and damp. A sense of foreboding came over Amartanon, but it was not a dangerous foreboding. It felt more like a slight apprehension over what was to come, coupled with the absolute certainty that all was as it should be. This was a feeling he had never before felt. It manifested as fear and as not-fear at the same time. Amartanon thought about the strangeness of this as he followed Mara deeper into the wood. He realized that the sense of fear growing in him as they ventured into the unknown added a sense of excitement and adventure to the experience. Without that sense of fear this experience would be boring…it would hold no interest for him. But the fear was not consuming him as it would have done in the past. It was now something he could dabble in; play with if he wanted. His fear no longer defined the situation; it flavored it. It occurred to him that he could embrace his fear as opposed to attempting to eliminate it, and by so doing he enhanced his enjoyment of the experience. This was new to him and he decided not to think about it too much. It seemed better to simply go with this experience, become one with it, and fully immerse himself in it. And somewhere in him he felt safe, detached from the fear, so that he was not paralyzed by it. It was a most pleasant feeling.

Mara pointed to a hill in the dark wood. "There is an entrance to a cave over there," he said. "I will go with you this time. I want to show you the unusual people who live there."

Amartanon looked into Mara's eyes and smiled. A tear formed in the corner of his right eye. It was a tear of absolute joy pushing forth, announcing its presence to the world. Amartanon was moving into a state of gratitude for life and everything in it *exactly as it is*. This gratitude had been missing before such that he constantly strove to change all that he thought was wrong in the world. Because of this he was utterly blind to the beauty of the valley *as it is*. But now he let go of wanting to alter the reality about him, and because of this the beauty of all came into clear view. He recognized that striving to change things was a good thing to do, so long as one did not invest in the outcome. He found that 'delicate poise,' that balance between wanting to make things better, and appreciating everything as it now is.

"Lead the way," he said, and as he did so he realized that he now trusted Mara completely. By this time, the idea of trust had been transformed in him as well. When fear is no longer a thing that happens to you, but is instead something you do to yourself so as to add excitement and adventure to whatever it is you are experiencing at the time, trust dissolves into something that is no longer dependent on the behavior of another, it is instead something Amartanon found to be always in him. Amartanon now saw that absolute acceptance of everything exactly as it is moved one to transcend the need for trust. It then occurred to him that trust is a concept used to deny the existence of fear. Only those ruled by fear believe themselves to need trust. He realized that if he needed to trust someone, that need already implied that he didn't trust them. It was an act of projecting on the other the state he wanted in himself. It was also an attempt to get from the other what he wanted, and trust therefore meant little more than the idea that the other would act in certain predictable ways. That form of trust was no trust at all. It was instead a judgment of the behavior of another until he reached that point where the behavior of the other comforted him. Trust is nothing but a word—a formation of sound attached to an idea. By resorting to trust, one binds oneself to fear by becoming a victim of it.

CHAPTER 10

"The entrance is right here," Mara said as he pointed to a small opening in the side of the hill. Mara lit the second torch. "Stay close to me," he instructed as he entered the cave, Amartanon followed close behind.

This cave was much like the previous one, Amartanon thought to himself. They walked slowly through a long, dark corridor, and soon the corridor opened into a large cavern. In the cavern were a strange people. There were all manner of machinery, test tubes, scientific looking instruments and the like. The people in the cave wore white lab coats and they scurried about busily performing various experiments, logging their observations on a computer. Amartanon stared at these people, and he noticed that they had no eyes. He whispered to Mara.

"What happened to their eyes?" he asked.

"There is no need to whisper," Mara replied. "Though they have ears, they do not hear in the same range as you and I. They can only hear sounds at a higher frequency. We can speak freely, and they will never know we are here."

"Ok," Amartanon said. "What happened to their eyes?"

"They are cave people," Mara answered. "They live their entire lives in the darkness of this cave. There is no light down here, so, they've lost the use of their eyes. You can still see the remnants of eyes, but you will notice that their eyelids have grown together so that their eyes cannot be opened. Surely you have heard of fish that live in caves that have lost their sight. Cave crickets cannot see either. It is the same for these people."

"Who are they?" Amartanon asked.

"I don't really know, but I like to call them Smartesians." Mara smiled thinking this funny. "They spend their lives down here performing all manner of experiments in an attempt to understand everything about the world. But they never leave the cave."

"Have they discovered everything there is to know?" Amartanon asked.

"They think so," Mara replied. "*But they have no eyes.* You see, they do not believe anything exists unless it can be empirically demonstrated to exist. *But they have no eyes.* They are very intelligent and they have created numerous mathematical equations that eloquently describe everything in the universe they are able to perceive. *But they have no eyes.* They've discovered incredibly complex and accurate descriptions of the universe. *But they have no eyes.* They don't even know eyes exist since they have never encountered any creature that has them. And their hearing is limited to a very narrow range. You see, to them we do not exist."

Amartanon observed the Smartesians, and indeed, they did not know the two existed, even though they wandered about in their midst.

"But what about all of the things in the world that they don't know exist?" Amartanon asked. "I mean, their inability to see something does not mean it is not there. Surely they must be able to detect things that people like you and I cause. Don't they seek those causes?"

"In a sense, they do," Mara replied. "But they look for patterns in the phenomena that they are able to detect, then they seek causes in that which they know to exist. The anomalies are then disregarded as mere errors in measurement."

"But I would think that they would be able to discover our existence even though they cannot see us," Amartanon protested.

"Really?" Mara answered. "Imagine one of the Smartesians telling the others that the anomalies of their observations are caused by living creatures that their senses cannot detect; that there is an entire civilization of these creatures existing in the universe and that learning more about them will further their understanding of the world. That Smartesian would be ridiculed for daring to suggest such a foolish thing. No, their entire universe is this cave, and everything they think they know is contained within it."

"Wow!" Amartanon said, not knowing what else to say.

"Watch this," Mara said, and he walked toward one of the Smartesians and touched him on the shoulder. Mara quickly stepped away as the Smartesian groped about in an attempt to find what had touched him.

"See," Mara said. "He felt something, now he is attempting to verify its existence by reassuring himself through his tactile senses that it really happened. Watch him."

Amartanon watched as the Smartesian groped about in an effort to find that which had touched his shoulder. Soon he shrugged his shoulders and abandoned the effort.

"Do you see what he just did?" Mara asked. "He could not find any cause for that which he experienced, and he has now convinced himself that it was just his imagination. He has removed it from his mind as if nothing real happened simply because he is unable to verify that something real *did* happen."

Mara continued, "This is the problem with materialism. Materialists arrogantly assume that the senses they know of are the only senses that exist. They think empirical data is absolutely objective, without realizing that empirical data is dependent upon the being making the observation. They believe themselves to be creating a complete and accurate description of the world, yet that description cannot include anything that does not come to them through their senses. They are really only describing that which is possible to describe according to the sensory data they are able to detect. Because of this, they cannot even ask the right questions. They cannot conceive of sight, therefore they have no idea that color exists. Because of this, they cannot ask questions related to color, or light, or wavelengths of light. All of that simply does not exist to these people. Yet they refer to the outcome of their experiments as empirical data, as if it is somehow objective, never realizing that the data they derive is completely dependent upon the questions they are able to ask. And the questions they are able to ask are dependent upon the senses they possess.

"Their world is this cave. They are trapped within it and they do not know they are trapped. They will never be able to create a complete description of reality, because they have no idea how their view of reality is limited. They refuse to believe anything exists unless it can be demonstrated to exist to them through their very limited sensory organs. They devise various machines so as to enhance their ability to detect things, but these machines are designed according to the senses they know to exist. For example, since they cannot imagine sight to exist, they have never thought to create a machine capable of detecting light. Those energy wavelengths are to them as if they do not exist. And yet they believe that they have described reality exactly as it is. It is a very arrogant assertion that the only senses that exist are those they possess. They don't realize that the thing they refer to as empirical evidence is nothing more than a form of subjective evidence that is dependent upon them. They think it objective when it is not."

"These are strange people," Amartanon said.

"Not so strange," Mara replied. "They are like all people. They resist the idea that anything exists unless their senses tell them it exists. There are literally thousands of different ways in which things can be perceived. You, my friend, think yourself to have only five senses. Because of this, you are very much like these Smartesians—trapped in a world where only that which you are able to directly perceive is thought to be real. How many times have you experienced something, just like my touching of the Smartesian, but when you went to look, you saw nothing there, so you dismissed it as if it was just your imagination? There is much more than you know, and you have the sensory apparatus to perceive it much like these Smartesians have eyes. But just as their eyes have atrophied from non-use, your other senses have atrophied from non-use. There are dimensions to this universe you cannot begin to imagine."

Amartanon watched these strange people as they went about describing the world exactly as it is, never realizing that the idea "exactly as it is" was an idea completely dependent upon them such that there never is an "exactly as it is." They were, in actuality, only describing reality to themselves in the peculiar manner in which they were able to perceive it.

"This then is their science?" Amartanon asked.

"It is," Mara answered. "But science has never been about discovering a reality that exists independently of the person doing the discovering. It has always been an interaction between the observer and the observed. Empirical data means nothing more than the data we are able to detect, detected in the manner in which our minds are able to process it, and interpreted by our subjective minds such that an arbitrary number of subjective interpretations agree. The fact that we cannot detect something in no way means that it does not exist. And the way that we find patterns and then organize those patterns so as to make sense of them is nothing more than the way our minds are capable of learning. Another mind from another species might organize information completely differently and thus be able to experience this universe in a way which we cannot. This is the important realization that people like the Smartesians simply do not know. They think themselves to have done away with faith entirely, yet their science is absolutely predicated on faith, the faith that only that which can be observed *by them* exists. Because of this, they are forever trapped in this cave."

Amartanon thought for a moment. "Why did you bring me here?"

Mara smiled. "So that you could begin to open the eyes you do not yet realize you have."

"How do I do that?"

"You stop doing what these Smartesians are doing. You stop accepting everything you have been taught. You question everything. You assume positions that you want to reject and consider the truth that might exist in them. You break the shackles of conditioned thinking so you can begin to think for yourself. You have never done this. Just like the Smartesians, most of your thinking has been done for you. It continues to be done for you though you believe you are doing it for yourself. It is by questioning everything that you begin to free yourself. You are every bit as trapped in a cave as these people, and like them, you do not know it."

Amartanon considered these words. He felt the desire to reject them as foolishness, yet he realized that this desire was a manifestation of the very conditioned thinking that kept him trapped. He decided then that he would drop his conditioned beliefs, and be open to that which he never imagined possible. He had no need to remain in the cave and he turned to leave, not waiting for Mara or the torch to light the way. He knew the way and had no need of anyone to guide him.

CHAPTER 11

"It is time," Mara said as they exited the cave, "to meet the one whom you've always desired to meet."

"And who might that be?" Amartanon asked.

"Why Jesus, of course," Mara answered as if surprised by the silliness of the question.

"Jesus?" Amartanon asked disbelievingly.

"Yes," Mara replied. "He is just around the next bend.

"You are taking me to meet Jesus?"

"I will lead you there; what you do once we arrive is up to you."

Amartanon thought to himself how ridiculous this was, and he began to think Mara had lost his mind. But as he was thinking this, they rounded the bend. There, spread out as far as the eye could see, were throngs of people. The two wandered amongst those who prostrated themselves, others singing hymns and praises, and still others chanting in homage to the Holy One. Amartanon made his way to the front of the crowd, and he did see there a man unlike any he had seen before. This man sat on a throne made of gold. He was a very large man; and even though he was seated Amartanon could tell he was at least ten feet tall. Upon his head was a crown of gold. Upon his face was a look of absolute kindness, compassion, love and joy. His radiance was of such brilliance that one had to shield one's eyes when looking upon him so as to give the eyes time to adjust to his brilliance. Amartanon felt his soul longing to be with the radiance of the Almighty One. He yearned to be one with this magnificent man. He felt love beyond love; joy beyond joy, and tears welled in his eyes. He and Mara approached the throne, and Amartanon stared deeply into the eyes of the Son of Man.

Amartanon barely noticed the tiny servant of the Son of Man as he returned having cleaned the chamber pot of the radiant one. The servant sat beside the Son of Man, tenderly washing his feet in holy reverence for this manifestation of God made flesh. Mara nudged Amartanon gently.

"Go on," he said. "Approach him. He has been waiting for you and is ready to speak with you now."

Amartanon, not knowing what to do, walked up to the great one, averted his eyes, and fell to his knees lying prostrate before him. Waves of overwhelming love and joy flooded over him, such was the power of the presence of the almighty one. "Lord," he said, "Before this moment I never knew you existed—though I thought I knew.

I beseech you, oh great one, to honor me in your presence so that I may ask you the greatest of all questions. I seek an audience with the one that men have for millennia called Jesus."

To which the beautiful voice replied, "It pleases me that you have come to see me."

Amartanon's head darted upward. He stared perplexed. For the reply did not come from the majestic one seated on the throne; it came instead from the tiny servant-man washing his feet. He stood speechless for a moment, a dumb look on his face—a look not unlike that of a monkey attempting to fit a square peg into a round hole. Then his senses returned.

"You speak for your Master?" he asked.

The servant-man smiled. "You could say that, I suppose."

"Why does he not speak for himself?" Amartanon asked.

The servant turned his head to gaze upon the glorious one seated upon the golden throne. "I suppose he would have answered had he thought you were speaking to him."

"But I *was* speaking to him," Amartanon protested. "I even called him by name."

"Oh, my mistake," the servant answered. "I thought I heard you say Jesus."

"I did," Amartanon replied.

"Then you are speaking to me."

Amartanon stared not knowing what to say. A question slowly formed in his mind. "This vast multitude is gathered here in worship of you?" he asked.

The servant smiled. "No," he said. "They are here to worship *him*. These people do not see me. They don't even know I exist."

"I don't understand," Amartanon said weakly. His heart sank, as if his world was on the verge of collapse.

The servant smiled and spoke, "I am the one known as Jesus," he said.

"But you cleaned this man's chamber pot. You sit before him washing his feet."

"You see me, yet you do not know me," the servant replied. "The man on this throne is but a reflection of the unified beauty that is this large mass of people. They are enamored with themselves, so, when they attempt to look at me—they see him."

"I don't understand," Amartanon said.

"Is it really that hard to understand?" the servant claiming to be Jesus asked. "This vast multitude of people want to see me. But to see me, they must first look past themselves. You must understand they *want* to see me—but not really. What they really seek is a representation of themselves as all-powerful, and beautiful, and glorious, and all the rest of that nonsense."

"But you are nothing but a servant."

"Exactly," Jesus replied smiling. "Who in their right mind would want to worship the one who cleans the chamber pot of humanity?"

"So you are the one we are supposed to worship?"

Jesus laughed. "Of course not," he said. "The truth be told, I never asked anyone to worship me. It was they who decided to do that. They want to be my children, when it is I who am their son. I asked them to accompany me; but they chose to pursue me instead."

"Pursue you in what way?"

"Now that is the question, is it not? The man seated upon this throne would not have answered you for the truth is he does not speak. He merely reflects the divine essence that exists collectively within them. He is a mirage, a distraction. Because of him, they do not see me at all. They seek salvation through a man as opposed to an essence. They want to be saved as if it is possible for one man to save another, hah! They want it done for them because they do not wish to do it themselves. To do it oneself means to accept full responsibility for one's self. And who wants to do that? This is why I am so very pleased that you have come to see me. And by that I do not mean 'come' as in you have journeyed here. By 'come' I mean you have developed the ability. You have *come to be able* to see me. You were not so blinded by the beauty of he who sits on the throne that you were unable to notice me. Even as I walked among them, the twelve saw *him* and failed to see *me*. It was the thirteenth, she was the one who saw me; therefore that which is thought to be the last, is and ever was the first. Without the thirteenth, who was really the first, I could never have been."

Amartanon did not know what to say.

"I see you are troubled," Jesus said to him. "Let us retire to a more comfortable place. The one seated upon this throne is confusing you. Turn your back to him and you will no longer be blinded by him. He is but a reflection of the true light. The true light is soft and warm; his light is harsh and hard on the eyes. Come. I will take you into my home and we will speak more there."

Amartanon did turn his back on the glorious one seated upon

the throne. As he did so, he felt the earth quake beneath him. He looked at the multitude as he was startled and afraid, but he saw that they did not feel the earth move. He wondered if he really felt it himself, or if perhaps he had imagined it. He did not yet know that it was up to him to claim it.

The servant-man—who called himself Jesus—handed Amartanon a large clay pot. "I want you to take this to the stream and fill it. When you have filled it carry it to my home. There I will be waiting, and there I will answer your questions."

Amartanon took the clay pot from him. "You are leaving this place?" he asked. "Who will tend to this great one in your absence?"

The servant-man smiled, "There are many others by many names," he replied. "Did you think me the only one?"

"I no longer know what to think," Amartanon replied.

"Ah!" the one calling himself Jesus exclaimed. "You are beginning to see."

"I don't understand," Amartanon said quizzically.

"You can never think your way into any solution," Jesus replied. "Although you believe you think your way to a solution; if you examine it closely, you will find no connection between the thought and the realization. Even when you are learning a mathematical procedure, you think and you think, and you study and then you study more. Your mind attempts to grasp the concept, yet it cannot. There suddenly comes this 'aha!' moment when you see. That 'aha!' moment never comes from thought. It never comes from your mind. It comes from another place entirely. Yet you *believe* it came from thought because thinking is what you were doing just before it came. You now say you no longer know what to think. This implies that you are reaching that boundary between what you think, and what is. The less you think, the more you will see. The more you see, the more you will know. The more you know the more you will realize that you do not know anything. It is the paradox of wisdom my friend, and your mind will never make sense of it. All truth is found in the contradiction such that anything that is found to be true is also not true. It is all a matter of perception."

Amartanon stared dumbfounded by this Jesus who spoke to him with such strange words. His mind wanted to understand the words, and even though he was troubled, he noticed something in this man that comforted him in his confusion. He became aware that it was this comfort most people sought. He was beginning to see that it is the *discomfort* of this man's words that led to a true repose—a repose that now seemed to hang in empty space just beyond his reach. To get there would require some act of faith beyond what Amartanon could imagine. He could no longer say how he knew these things— he could only say that he was beginning to know them.

"Where is your home that you speak of?" Amartanon asked.

"Mara will guide you there," Jesus answered.

"Then I will take this jar and I will fill it. I will journey to your home to meet you as you have asked of me," Amartanon said. The servant-man—who called himself Jesus—smiled, turned and walked away.

"Come," Mara said. "Let us climb to the top of this hill."

SOPHOS

"But we are in search of water," Amartanon replied. "Should we not seek it at the bottom of the hill?"

"Not this water," Mara replied. And with that Mara led the way, Amartanon following wherever Mara should take him. He no longer felt any need to move in any direction of his own will, of his own accord. He now sensed that he had always been travelling wherever Mara led, even when he thought it was he who was leading.

The two approached the top of the hill, and there a spring did issue forth. This surprised Amartanon as he saw the water flowing from this source, yet it travelled no more than a few feet down the hillside before the ground swallowed it, returning it to the source.

"This is the water that you must take to the man with whom you just spoke," Mara said. Amartanon filled his jar, then Mara led him down the hill, and then he led him down farther. They continued down and down, deeper than Amartanon imagined this valley could go. They descended to a place so deep that the light of the sun could no longer reach them. They pressed on deeper into the darkness. Amartanon was amazed that, though there was no longer any light to guide them, they found their way with no difficulty. Soon they had descended so far down that the air no longer moved—not the slightest of breezes could be felt upon the skin. The silence grew to a deafening roar. Amartanon thought for a moment that they would soon enter the gates of hell itself so deeply had they penetrated into the unknown and unknowable. But as soon as this thought came into his mind, it left him. He now saw his thoughts clearly as they travelled through his mind like clouds on the wind. He remembered

161

the time—not so long ago—when he clung to these thoughts turning them into his reality. He felt the old, familiar sensation of dis-ease as he was tempted to cling to each thought, but he recognized this as yet another thought and he did not cling to that temptation either. He remembered the words of the servant-man that nothing could be realized through thought; and he now saw, in the darkness of no light, the illusion of the reality he could create if he were to cling to any of these thoughts.

He then came to an astounding realization. The awareness came to him that fear is derived from thought, at the same time that fear creates the thought from which it is derived. He felt in his very bones the reality that the two come into existence as one. With that, he made a determination (or perhaps he made no determination at all), yes, that was it—a determination was simply made, there was no "he" making it. He no longer sought to imagine himself as the cause of the determination. The determination simply was. It came to be, though it always was and had forever been. The realization that simply happened in this thing he thought of as himself, was that letting go of thought was like letting go of one end of a stick of which fear was the other end. When you drop the one, the other falls with it. It mattered not which end he dropped first for they both went together—went away from him, for they had in his mind become him, and they were him no more.

Mara smiled, and Amartanon knew he was smiling though he had no way of knowing how he knew this. In the darkness he could not see, he could only feel the presence of the smile. The distance that he always thought separated him from others had dissolved such that he and other were meaningless words. Mara had become an extension of Amartanon even as he was other than Amartanon, as all people had become extensions of him as well.

"It would seem that we have arrived," Mara said, but as there was no longer any air to carry the sound, Amartanon had no way of knowing how he heard this. He was in a state of total awareness. He reached out his hand and found a door which he opened, a door that he knew would be there though he didn't know how he knew this. He was using some sensory apparatus that he never knew he had. Unlike the Smartesians he had met in the cave, he no longer ignored that which came to him from senses of which he was not aware he possessed. He now let that input into his mind and accepted it as being as real as any other sensory input. As such, awareness simply came to him and he trusted that it was not imagination, it was instead a part of the reality that had always been, the reality he had forever been immersed in though he never knew it. He and Mara then stepped inside.

"Welcome to my home," a voice said. And as the words were spoken, Jesus appeared before him, light emanating from him. They stood in a tiny wooden hut, an abode so simple that it seemed as if it was but was not. It was built out of rotting wood; the floor nothing but wooden planks unevenly spaced, so old and rotted from neglect that they felt spongy beneath his feet. Amartanon thought to himself that this hut had once been a beautiful palace, but had deteriorated with age and shrank to such an extent that there was only this small remnant of it remaining, and that which remained would not be here long. A woman sat on the floor on the right side of Jesus, his right hand placed upon her shoulder, and her right hand placed on the floor beneath them. Amartanon immediately knew this to be the thirteenth Jesus spoke of earlier.

Jesus spoke, "You have come."

Amartanon replied, "I never knew you to be," he said. "I certainly never thought I would find you, of all people, here."

"It had to be me," Jesus said.

"Why?" Amartanon asked.

"Because this is the form you came to know. Had you been another person born in another place or time, I might have been another. But for you, it had to be me." Jesus stared into Amartanon's eyes, and he felt himself comforted. "Place the jar on the floor here between us," he said.

Amartanon did as he was instructed, and as he did so, the jar dissolved through the rotted floor, the floor dissolving with it so that the hand of the woman sitting beside Jesus now touched the earth itself. From this woman a light did begin to shine; a light drawn from the earth itself, bright, but pleasing to the eyes. It shone a bluish-white, travelling up her arm, through her body and into Jesus. This caused the light of Jesus to shine brighter than before. Water began to flow into a tiny stream that issued forth from the place where the jar was laid.

"As it is above, so it must also be below," Jesus said, and the water did flow with greater intensity, forming into streams that flowed up rather than down. Amartanon now knew that this water would flow up into the valley and it would begin to nourish the people there.

"Welcome Water-Bearer. All hail the Water Bearer," Jesus said smiling with admiration for the man standing before him.

Amartanon simply stared not knowing what to say. He felt as if he had wandered into a dream, and he no longer knew what was real and what was unreal. His body felt a subtle yet distinct energy, as though he were sensing something that transcended his usual senses. But this he reflexively ignored, thinking it nothing but a figment of his imagination. As he did so, he became aware of doing so, and he said to himself, "No! I will not ignore this." He then felt that energy growing strong within him, permeating every fiber of his being. He began to glow. He glanced at the woman upon whom Jesus' hand rested. For an instant she seemed to exist in two places at once—on the floor with Jesus' hand on her shoulder, and above him, her hands resting on him. He blinked, and when he did so, there was only the one image of the woman kneeling on the floor. The thought that he had seen anything other left his mind before he was fully aware that the thought ever existed—such that the thought was in his mind at the same time that it never was. He chased after the thought in the periphery of his awareness and caught it. He willed it into him, into his awareness such that he could now know. The woman was in both places at once as she was the essence of Jesus in another form. A distant fear cried out in the darkness, but this too he allowed in, and as he did so, the fear vanished into the ether. All of this flashed in his mind in a fraction of a second, and it was no more—as if it never happened, so to him, it never happened though to him, it did.

Mara knelt beside Amartanon, and without any thought, Amartanon dropped his left hand to Mara's shoulder mirroring Jesus and the woman. It was a gesture that provided him a feeling of comfort in this most strange and unusual place. Mara reached down and touched the earth. The servant-man—who called himself Jesus—smiled.

"You have questions for me?" Jesus asked.

Amartanon paused to gather his thoughts. Where he had been filled with questions only a moment before, he now struggled to remember what they were.

"Relax," Jesus said. "Take a seat and breathe. You are safe here."

A chair appeared behind Amartanon and he sat, his hand never leaving Mara's shoulder. His mind settled. His body grew calm. He realized there was nothing to fear.

"I journeyed from atop the great mountain," he said. "I came to teach that which I had learned."

Jesus asked, "How can you teach that which you do not know?"

"But I do know it," Amartanon protested. "It came to me in a vision."

"The vision is but the beginning," Jesus answered, his voice soft and calm. "You cannot know a thing through thought. You must experience it in your body before it can become real. You merely caught a glimpse of that which you have not as yet experienced. That glimpse will only carry you so far."

"I don't understand…"

"An experience of the mind," Jesus interrupted, "that is not informed by the heart, is no experience at all. It is but an abstraction, a description of the experience. The heart thinks just as the mind thinks. It is the division between heart and mind that causes strife. When the two think in unison, then you will know peace."

"Hearts do not think," Amartanon protested.

"That depends," Jesus replied. "The heart informs the thought of the mind with that which is beyond the ability of the mind to comprehend."

"But people who follow their hearts wander foolishly about in this world in denial of the reality around them."

Jesus' eyes grew bright. "That is true," he said. "The heart detached from the grounding influence of the mind is as lost as the mind wandering blindly without the visions of the heart. You must unlearn all that you think you know, so that all can be learned again with the guiding influence of the heart. To do less, is to do nothing."

"I still don't understand."

Jesus leaned forward in his chair. He dipped his hand in the water issuing forth from the ground. "This water will quench the thirst, but it cannot yet cure the hunger." He looked up at Amartanon. "You came here to teach that which you have learned?" he asked.

"I did," Amartanon answered.

"You wanted to share with the world all that you had come to know?"

"Yes."

"And who has learned anything since you have been here?" he asked.

Amartanon stared blankly. "I've tried to teach many, but none wanted to listen. They already think they know."

"I see," Jesus replied. "And what is it they think they know?"

"They see images of themselves that are not what they really are. They do strange things without knowing why they do them. And then there was Solon who told me God is the Devil and the Devil is God."

"I see," Jesus replied. "You saw the idealist who did not see value in the material world, the materialist who has no appreciation for anything his senses do not report to him, and you saw the ascetic who cannot see the harm he does to himself?"

"Yes…and Solon."

"And Solon who thinks God is the Devil and the Devil is God. And you say that these people learned nothing from you because they could not listen to anything you had to teach?

"That's right."

"I wonder…what did you learn from them?"

Amartanon grew defensive. "I came here to teach them, not to learn from them," he said.

"You thought you would teach them without first learning from them so that you could benefit from whatever it is they had to teach you?" Jesus asked.

"You are not making sense," Amartanon protested.

Jesus took a deep breath and leaned back in his chair. "I am not so sure who it is that sees only illusions reflected in the mirror," he said. "But no matter. Solon is a good friend of mine. He has something of value to offer you."

SOPHOS

"But he said that God is the Devil and he even said that you are Lucifer."

"These are just words," Jesus answered sternly, his tone surprising Amartanon. His voice then softened. "You must try to see beyond them. What if the God of the Old Testament was the Devil? What if my teachings were exactly that? Did you take the time to consider what those particular words would add to your understanding?"

Amartanon shook his head in disbelief. "Am I to believe that you are Lucifer? I'm not sure I really believe you are Jesus."

"Can you consider an argument without accepting it or rejecting it? Can you simply play with it without judging it through your preconceived ideas?" Jesus asked.

This surprised Amartanon as he had never thought of such a thing before. "I don't know," he said. "I suppose I could try."

Jesus' eyes narrowed and he leaned toward Amartanon. "If you reject any teaching without considering it, you can learn nothing. If you learn nothing, then there is nothing for you to teach. For teaching is an interaction, not a dissertation. You must unravel the words you use if you are to find the essence they represent. You must learn to communicate with others while recognizing that the root of the word 'communicate' is to commune. This implies an intimacy in which the two are acting together for the benefit of both. You communicate through conversation, the root of that word being the same as conversion. You are both converted in your thinking through the interaction. Any interaction between two people is very

169

much like a chemical reaction in which both substances are utterly transformed into something completely new. If you deny yourself this experience, then you never truly communicate with anyone. You simply talk at them as opposed to conversing with them. You must abandon this idea you have of a solid self. You are a fluid thing, forever changing, forever molding the environment in which you exist as you are molded by it. You think yourself to have been born into sin, but do you know the original meaning of that word? It is the Greek word 'hamartia,' it means to miss the mark. Because you have missed the mark, you are disconnected from that essence you know as God, for God is the mark you missed. Another Greek word for sin is 'agnoeema' meaning ignorance when one should have known. You then turn to religion, derived from the Latin word 'religare' meaning to bind together or connect. You must religion yourself, or reconnect yourself to that which you missed, or to that which you should have known.

"Solon knows this about words. That is why he has a way of saying things that challenge your assumptions. It is these assumptions, carried in your mind as words, that stand in your way of true realization. I never said I was the son of God, though many misunderstood me and took my words to mean just that. I did say that I was a Son of God. To be *a* Son of God is a far different thing from being *the* Son of God. I rarely used the word God, however, because I found that word to be wanting. God is the most dangerous word ever invented by man because it hides from the mind the very thing it promises to represent. I decided instead to use the word Father. The Father is above and beyond God, and yet God, you, me, everything in the universe is in the Father. The Father is in you as he is in me. Calling the being you know as God the Devil, is an attempt to help you make that connection. It isn't like God *is* the Devil. Calling me Lucifer is another way of getting you to look at what you have always thought to be evil in a different light. You must turn everything around, stand it on its head, and consider it in terms of its opposite before you can claim to know anything. To do less is simply to accept what you have been taught without considering the truth of what you have been taught. You must think for yourself and stop listening to those ideas you have accepted without critical examination." His voice carried an unwavering authority.

"I still don't understand," Amartanon protested.

"You are resisting. Unless you come to me as a little child, you cannot know me."

"What are you talking about?"

"Children have no preconceived ideas. I am trying to free you from your preconceptions. You are blind! You do not know who you are. You do not even know *where* you are."

"What do you mean by that? I am here in the valley."

"Are you?" Jesus asked.

"Of course I am," Amartanon replied. "Where else would I be?"

"There is no valley!" Jesus snapped. "There never was a valley. You violated your own wisdom when you entered here and you have learned nothing because you think you already know. You know nothing!" Jesus stood and approached Amartanon. He leaned toward him and whispered in his ear.

"You see me as a man named Jesus. I am not a man. I am an essence; the Christ essence that exists within you. You think you are in the valley, but you are not. What you think of as the valley is actually your own heart. And here, in the deepest, darkest recesses of your heart, in that most hidden of the hidden places, you found...me."

Terror surged from the depths of Amartanon's being. His body convulsed in response. He panted and gasped for breath. The world before his eyes spun wildly so he closed them tightly in a vain attempt to keep out that which was now flooding into his awareness. He struggled to deny the reality of the experience, to make it go away. But it was as if a balloon had burst and there was no going back. He had but one option—to push through. His mind strained to the point where he thought it might snap, abandoning him forever in the depths of insanity. He wanted to run, to scream, to hide, yet his body no longer responded to the commands of his thoughts. Fear swelled into an absolute panic. Just when he thought all was lost, a voice whispered in his ear.

"Relax and breathe," the voice said reassuringly. He had heard this voice before; the voice of a woman. "I am with you," it whispered. "Let yourself fall into me."

Amartanon did let go of the last resistance of his body, surrendered to his fear and began to breathe. The world spinning around him slowed. Warmth enveloped him and his panic subsided, first into a mild fear, next an ephemeral anxiety, then it left him completely. The room grew quiet and still. He opened his eyes.

He felt his eyes burn and he squinted reflexively in response to the bright light shining all around him. His breath slowed from panting gasps to a steady rhythm. As his eyes adjusted to the light, he saw that he was no longer in the small shack in the depths of the valley. He looked about and saw that he was standing in a room, his arms, legs and neck shackled with chains preventing all movement. He could not even turn his head, so thoroughly was he bound. He scanned the room and saw that it opened into a large expanse. He saw before him a waist-high railing, and on the other side were benches upon which people sat watching him. Between he and the people was an abyss yawning into the nothingness between them. To his left, he saw Mara, to his right was the servant-man who called himself Jesus.

A voice boomed from behind him. "Here stands the man charged with being less than what he is," the voice said, and Amartanon immediately recognized it as the voice of God. The voice continued, "This man thinks himself to be God. How dare any man think such a thing?" The voice was dreadful, and Amartanon knew that his soul was on trial. The heavy chains tied about him seemed to be pulling him into the abyss of annihilation before him. He strained against them. He knew that if he let himself go they would drag him into the nothingness that spread out beneath his feet; his existence contained in his resistance to the weight of the chains.

He wondered how long he had been bound like this. Though it seemed that he only now appeared here, another part of him knew that he had been bound like this forever. The voice behind him spoke again, "Let the accuser speak to the charges against this man," it boomed.

Mara stepped forward. "This is the man," he cried out, and Amartanon stared at Mara surprised that his voice was so loud and forceful. "He is the one who dared think himself God. He is the man who climbed the mountain and became so full of himself that he thought himself the one above all. He violated Sophia in his haste to teach that which he does not know. He is the blasphemer! He is the heretic! He is the one who refuses to conform. He is vile and wicked. His soul deserves the punishment of absolute annihilation. This Man is an abomination! No Man is above the law! No Man is above the very God who created him. He is a devil and must be punished for his sins. Into the pit he should go."

Amartanon's eyes grew wide in disbelief. He did not understand how such accusations could be levied against him, and by Mara of all people. He felt himself betrayed. The audience shouted insults and cried out for justice. "Put this man to death!" they shouted with angry eyes that pierced the very depths of his soul.

"Let the advocate speak," the voice behind him thundered.

The servant-man Jesus stepped forth. "This man is kind and good," he said softly, compassionately. "He meant well in all that he has done. His soul is filled with love, and no soul filled with love deserves to be destroyed. Any fault you may find in him is not of his own doing. He is but the product of the world in which he lived. How can anyone in this room find fault in him that does not also exist in each and every one of you? This man deserves our compassion and our understanding. Let us not be so quick to condemn him." It was an impassioned plea that served to silence the spectators who only a moment before were calling for his death.

The voice behind him spoke again. "What say ye, man? What is your answer to the charges levied against you?"

The room grew deathly silent. All in attendance waited to hear what this man had to say. His eyes looked to his left at Mara. Then he looked to his right toward Jesus. He glanced down at the chains that bound him and he stared into the abyss stretching out beneath him. It was then that he remembered the words spoken to him not so very long ago.

"You see a man where there is only an essence," he remembered, and he looked to the man Jesus who had said this to him. Jesus, sensing this, smiled. For Jesus knew himself to be acting as a man in this proceeding, whereas the essence he represented was something more—something other.

Amartanon stared at the spectators. He saw sitting there Sophia, crying in anguish, longing to save Amartanon from himself, all the while knowing she could not. He saw too the white cat now beside Sophia, her right hand gently stroking the animal. Sophia seeing him staring at her stood. She crossed through the opening in the railing separating Amartanon from the others. She glided across the abyss as if it was not there. She approached Amartanon and kissed him ever so gently on the cheek. As she whispered in his ear, he recognized hers as the voice that had earlier comforted him. "It is not for you to discover who you are," she whispered softly, "It is for you to claim that which you already know yourself to be."

With that she stepped back and stood before him hovering over the abyss, her eyes pleading with him to see that which he had never before seen. Amartanon knew that she knew what he did not. He stared into her. Then he looked at Mara. It was in that moment that he began to see at last. The hidden thing was never hidden. It was so close to him that he had always looked past it. For it was not other than him. It was, and always had been, exactly what it was now—him.

Amartanon smiled. The faces in the crowd before him grew fearful. They sensed that this man was something other than what any man before him dared to be. Amartanon looked down at the chains that bound him, and commanded the chains to dissolve into the nothingness they had always been. The chains thus faded, and were no more. It was then that Amartanon spoke.

"I am the man who climbed the great mountain," he said. "And it is I who travelled to the valley below to teach that which I had learned. For I was both teacher and student. I had much to learn from that which I thought I had already learned. The valley was the valley of my heart—the mirror that at every moment reflected back to me that which I was but did not know myself to be. You, advocate, the man known as Jesus, you are but a parody that exists only in my mind. As advocate, you also offer excuses—and it is the excuses you offered for my ignorance that kept me bound to your image. This my heart knew, but my mind knew not. I had to purge the image so I might find the essence, the true essence that is you, living inside of me.

"And you adversary known as Mara. You are but a parody of the essence that is you as well. You accuse me of such terrible things, binding me forever to my guilt and my shame. Yet it is you that drove me on. Without you I would have had no reason to search and to find. So it was that the very thing I thought would save me hindered me, while that which I thought would condemn me freed me. You and Jesus are both nothing but mirrors that exist nowhere but in my mind. I now command you to dissolve into the essence that you truly are."

With that, Jesus and Mara did begin to dissolve. And as they did so, the essences of them both floated through the room toward Sophia. It was in Sophia that the two did merge into the essence that they had always been such that Amartanon now saw that it was Sophia who had been guiding him all along.

"And you, woman," Amartanon continued, "are but a parody as well. You, the reflection of all that I am and of all that I can be as I am but the reflection of you. For you are me, as I am you. Merge into me now as I merge myself into you." And the two, man and woman, did dissolve into their respective essences, and those essences intermingled into one, danced about the room, then they returned such that they stood as two manifestations of the one— one the man; the other the woman, both the same manifestation of a unified essence. Sophia walked to the man and took his hand, the abyss closing beneath her, and the essence of the two now pulsed in rhythm together as one heart beating in the darkness of the brightly lit room. Amartanon looked into her eyes and did see himself reflected there, as she saw herself reflected in his. He smiled. She smiled with him.

"Shall we?" he asked.

"Let it be done," she answered, and the two turned to face the God standing in judgment behind them. Sophia knelt beside Amartanon as he stood before his God. Sophia's left hand touched the earth beneath them drawing from it her strength which she channeled into him through her right hand placed upon the small of his back. The two fused into a unity unlike any the world had ever witnessed before.

"And you," Amartanon said with the authority bestowed upon him by the woman kneeling beside him. "What a tiny little God you are," he said. "You dare stand in judgment of *me*? It is *I* who will now stand in judgment of *you*. For you are nothing but a parody of the true God, the Father. It is the Father that transcends every concept of a God that the mind of man might create or imagine. *You* were created in *my* image. I was never created in yours. The Father is in me as I am in the Father. You hold no dominion here and your court is a court of fools. It is you who is and always was the ultimate fool. I now deny you, for you are nothing but a creation—a fantasy, created by me, for me. You have no authority over me. We have now eaten of the fruit of the tree, and we have become like you and we see you for what you are. You feared me, as I have feared you. This woman who was with me all along though I knew it not inspired me to do it, and we have no need of you now! I was, as this woman said I was, Amartanon, the fool. But now my name is Sophos, the wise."

Thunder roared and the earth quaked beneath them. The walls shook and the people in the courtroom cowered in fear. Sophos and Sophia stood as the proclamation of that which they chose to be in defiance of the God who wished to deprive them of it. The God before them cried out and the heavens fell as this God dissolved into nothing, for this God was nothing but the man's own ego projected back to himself as God. The man and woman, together, had gone beyond God into the pure essence of the Father who was also the Mother. With this act the room dissolved into nothing and the man found himself standing on the mountain from which his journey began. "I am Sophos the wise, and this is Sophia, the source of all my strength, all my power." Sophia stood by his side as the two, standing as one, stared out across the great expanse. The cat shone a brilliant white and glowed as it purred while rubbing first upon his leg, then upon hers in a figure-eight motion between the two that united them as one and bound them inexorably together. He looked into her mind with his eyes and he spoke without words, spoke into her being as she spoke into his.

"I am the mind," he said.

"And I am the heart," she replied.

The two now knew that they balanced one another, that the one was nothing without the other. A mind without a heart is a machine—a heart without a mind is a fool. And the two, standing together, realized the deepest of the mysteries. That in their union they did give birth to the One—thus the torch was passed, and the new age did dawn.

———

This is the un-telling of the story as I promised I would un-tell it. I, a mere mortal, bore witness and do hereby attest that everything happened just as I have reported it to you. I witnessed the birth of Sophos the Water-Bearer, and into this world he has come. The age of Pisces is thus ended and the age of Aquarius has arrived. Sophos no longer travels in the valley; he instead expresses from the valley as he travels in this world. His water flows so that all who drink of it will not only have their thirst quenched, but also their hunger sated. It is the rejuvenating water that is the elixir of life—true life, eternal life. I have un-told the story to you as it was un-told to the Water-Bearer himself. And this is my gift to you that you may find the Water-Bearer who, as the essence that he is, exists in us all.

THE OTHER SIDE OF HELL

Be sure and get your copy of Charles Bynum's first book "The Other Side of Hell. This is the story of the fall into the darkness of addiction and the journey out the other side. This is a must read if you or someone you know is dealing with addiction or if you have a family member who is struggling. This book has helped many people recover and to create for themselves a new life better than before.

You can read Charles' blog at www.charles-bynum.blogspot.com. Be sure to check out his website at www.charlesbynum.com.

ABOUT THE AUTHOR

Charles Bynum is a philosopher, public speaker and author. Understanding the human condition through psychology, sociology and philosophy interests him. The condition of the world that surrounds us inspires and influences his work. He is an author whose work is a blend of fiction and fact that is most often expressed in prose, but he also writes poetry, and has recently published a personal account of an experience in human tragedy. Charles seeks an understanding of the political landscape and each member's personal responsibility toward the future of our society.

Charles brings his powerful message to others in the community. He volunteers at the local military base helping soldiers who return from deployment with PTSD and substance abuse issues. He also works with the Teen Court helping kids who have lost their way. His unique approach to these issues is healing to those in need. Charles also lectures regularly at colleges where he speaks to psychology and criminal justice students so as to teach his approach to others who will themselves be working with people who are suffering.

His message is inspiring, moving and life-altering. Charles offers insights into the human condition that affect us all. His words reach deeply into the depths of the human psyche—that of existential despair—and from those depths he brings to his audience a path out of the darkness. It is a message of hope, a message of joy, a message that conveys the beauty that is life.

You can find his web site at www.charlesbynum.com.

www.ingramcontent.com/pod-product-compliance
Lightning Source LLC
Chambersburg PA
CBHW070957040426
42443CB00007B/545